The Incidental Guru

The Incidental Guru

Lessons in Healing from a Dog

Keith, Continue to confound—nue on Continue on the healing Journey, the spirit lives the spirit gives the spirit

CINDY STONE

Love and many blessings,
Cindy Stone

Love, Harry

WINDING STAIR PRESS

cindystone@incidentalguru.com

NATIONAL LIBRARY OF CANADA CATALOGUING
IN PUBLICATION DATA

Stone, Cindy
    The incidental guru : lessons in healing from a dog

Includes bibliographical references.
ISBN 1-55366-241-5

1. Dogs—Therapeutic use. 2. Human-animal relationships.
I. Title.

BF637.S4S828 2002   636.7   C2002-900259-1

Winding Stair Press
An imprint of Stewart House Publishing Inc.
290 North Queen Street, #210
Etobicoke, Ontario M9C 5K4
Canada
1-866-574-6873
www.stewarthouse.com

Executive Vice President and Publisher: Ken Proctor
Director of Publishing and Product Acquisition: Joe March
Production Manager: Ruth Bradley-St-Cyr
Developmental Editing: Lisa Proctor
Copy Editing: Judy Phillips
Text Design: Laura Brady
Cover Design: Sari Naworynski
Cover Photo: José Crespo

This book is available at special discounts for bulk purchases by groups
or organizations for sales promotions, premiums, fundraising and edu-
cational purposes. For details, contact: Stewart House Publishing Inc.,
Special Sales Department, 195 Allstate Parkway, Markham, Ontario
L3R 4T8. Toll free 1-866-474-3478.

1 2 3 4 5 6 07 06 05 04 03 02

Printed and bound in Canada by Transcontinental Printing

Table of Contents

Acknowledgements / vii

Preface / xi

Elements of Healing: The Unexpected Source / 1

Harry on Courage: Fear Rules If You Let It! / 25

Harry on Trust: A Two-Way Street / 78

Harry on Respect: Honor Yourself and Others / 111

Harry on Love: More Than Give and Take / 150

The Lessons Continue / 190

Suggested Reading / 216

To my mother, Rene, who through her absence shaped my life, and to Adam Stone who saved Harry from an uncertain future.

Acknowledgments

I CANNOT POSSIBLY THANK all the people who have touched my life in such ways that contributed to this book. It would not have been possible but for the incredible help I received from my friends and family. My sister, Wendy, who is the closest experience to unconditional love that anyone could imagine, believed unquestioningly in me and in Harry's ability to transform his wild ways to become a wonderful dog. My brother-in-law, David, made sure I was always well fed with plenty of red wine. My nephew, Maxx, brought energy and joy to my life. My brother, Nick, busy developing his own career, made time to keep our close connection thriving. My stepdaughter, Sarah, is always full of love, encouragement, and acceptance. My father, Len, is an inspiration with his incredible recovery from open-heart surgery. My paternal grandfather and grandmother, long departed, are still felt.

A special thanks goes to Dr. Evelynn Sommers. During the

early stages of the book, Evelynn tirelessly read my manuscripts and constantly challenged me to think deeper, questioned my assumptions, and was instrumental in helping me shape the material into its present form. She has been a wonderful friend to both Harry and me.

Thanks to everyone at Stewart House Publishing, especially Joe March for believing in the project and making it a reality, and Ralph Peter. To my editor, Lisa Proctor, who not only helped to clarify and organize my ideas but also gave me encouragement to make it through the final stages of writing, and to my copy editor, Judy Phillips, for her wonderful attention to detail. Many thanks to the design team that made the book look so wonderful: Laura Brady, text design; Sari Naworynski, cover design; and José Crespo, cover photo.

Thanks to my dear friends, Cindy, Don, Ivan, Martin, Virginia, Anik, Lisa, Deborah, Graham, Megan, Alan, Clifford, Bryan, Dean, Vivien, Barb, Shelly, Abe, Marvin, Jeffrey, Fiona and Natalie, who tolerate my obsessions with gentle amusement. Thanks to Sheila and Ziggy for their generosity and for use of their cabin in the woods, which offered refuge whenever I needed it. I am truly blessed with so many special friends. Thanks to the friendships that have not always been easy or successful, for those are the friendships I have often learned the most from.

Thanks to Dr. Harry Prosen and the Milwaukee Zoo for allowing me to share their healing work with primates.

Thanks to Jennifer Beale for taking the journey with me. There were times!

Thanks to all of my clients over the years who have allowed me into their lives and souls, they made a difference to me and I hope I made a difference to them.

Thanks to my teachers from the past, and the present, to Adam Stone, to James Burn, and to Alex Kozma, for your love and friendship and for being all that you are.

"There is no use trying," said Alice; "one can't believe impossible things."

"I dare say you haven't had much practice," said the Queen. "When I was your age, I always did it for half an hour a day. Why, sometimes I've believed as many as six impossible things before breakfast."

— LEWIS CARROLL, from *Alice in Wonderland*

Preface

As a child, i had always wanted my own dog, but instead, I was allowed a succession of turtles; each I named Debbie, and each I gave an elaborate funeral with a pink tissue-lined chocolate box for a casket when it died. I also had a mouse named Ruby. I loved my little pets, but I really wanted more.

Our family dog was a black-and-dirty-white American spaniel which was rarely allowed in the house and rarely found in our yard, as he regularly scaled the fence to go on walkabouts that could last up to several weeks. My older sister was given by our grandparents a white toy-sized poodle she named Barney. Our neighbors and my second family, Bernice and Reg, and their three boys, had Labrador hunting dogs, Shadow and Dory. I, too, wanted a dog of my own.

I read the novel *White Fang* in grade school, and it made a profound impression on me. It is the story about a working dog who was first owned by a gentle man, then stolen by a gambler, who tormented the dog into becoming an aggressive fighter for the ring, then found by a boy who transformed the fearful, aggressive dog into a loving pet. I adored the story and devoured every book I could get my hands on that took me into the depths of the wilderness and the lives of animals. I lived for the times our family would go camping in the woods and the northern lake regions. I fancied myself a naturalist and thought it would be my life. It is funny how much of our later lives are shaped by these kinds of influences.

My fascination with the dynamics of relationships broadened to human relationships when I studied sociology at the University of Toronto. I became an art therapist, learning a great deal about children, adolescents, and child development. Later I went on to a master's degree in psychology and studied with several wonderful mentors, Dr. H. Freedman, M.D., D. of Psych., F.R.C.P.; Dr. P. Brawley, M.D., D. of Psych., F.R.C.P.; and J. Golden, M.S.W., O.A.M.F.T., each whom influenced the way I practiced psychotherapy.

In my practice, I found satisfaction in delving into personal relationships, being midwife to people's souls, and helping my clients discover their authentic selves. In my own life, I found satisfaction riding horses and in my involvement with social issues, and I found spiritual growth in the practice of ba gua chang, a Taoist internal martial art similar to tai chi. It is a Taoist meditation as well as a martial art that cultivates internal energy, relaxation, and healing.

It is said that when the student is ready, the teacher finds the student. That day at the pound when Harry found me, the story from my childhood came full circle. Like the boy in *White Fang*, the transformation of Harry from an aggressive dog that bites into a loving pet became somewhat of an obsession for me. I was compelled to understand Harry in the deepest way I possibly could. I was committed from the moment I discovered that with the help of Adam Stone, the canine aggression expert, I might possibly make a difference in Harry's life. Perhaps it was my psychotherapy training that led me to believe that change is possible and to be endlessly fascinated with what Harry's behavior might mean. The more I learned about Harry's behavior and dog behavior, the more I learned about my own.

At the time of Harry's rehabilitation, there seemed to be weekly stories in the newspapers about vicious dog attacks. Strangers at the beach, without asking, would toss Harry balls to chase and cookies to eat. That was when I decided I had to write about what I was learning from Harry. I wanted to share my newfound knowledge about the seriousness and the proliferation of dog aggression. It eventually became clear to me that what I was learning from Harry was applicable to all relationships, including human relationships.

Hiking on the Bruce Trail with my good friend, Clifford Shearing, the world-renowned criminologist and theorist on governance, our conversations traversed many worlds, while Harry, giddy with freedom, raced around the woods. It was the days of hiking and talking with Clifford that gave birth to the possibility of me writing this book. We were both undergoing transformations. Clifford was moving away from the structure of academics, moving from theorizing about making a difference to actualizing the theories he had been advancing by creating community restorative justice programs around the world, based on the culture and values of the indigenous people. And on my transformational journey I had discovered an intellectual, emotional and spiritual freedom that I wanted to share with others.

At times during the writing of this book, I feared being so open and vulnerable about who I really am. I wanted to erase it all and begin a different book, one where I could remain anonymous and guarded, one where I would reflect someone with incredible strength, fortitude, wisdom, and courage, someone with absolutely no vulnerabilities.

But we are all works in progress. We are all in the process of becoming. And I am no different. I am far from perfect. I struggle daily with my lessons and I don't always win. This book is a personal journey for me and, I hope, for the reader. A journey that will shine a light into the shadows of our being and open some doors that may have remained previously unnoticed.

Elements of Healing:
The Unexpected Source

I trust that everything happens for a reason, even
when we are not wise enough to see it.

—OPRAH WINFREY

IT WAS A CRISIS OF fear. Harry, my one-of-a-kind Disney dog
with the too large ears, scraggly wiry hair, and beard like an
Asian sage sat smartly at my feet. His topaz-colored eyes glanced
furtively past me towards his food bowl. Harry nuzzled me for
attention. I rubbed his ears. He nuzzled me again. Then he sat
back and growled, a low growl that quickly rose in pitch. His eyes
darkened. He crinkled his nose, lifting the folds of skin around
his black lips to reveal stunningly white, sharp, big teeth. In an
instant his normally benign canine looks metamorphosed into a
menacing wolfish grin. I took a deep breath in an effort to appear
physically imposing and quell the fear that was rising. "NO!" I
yelled, "Bad dog!" I reached out for his collar and Harry — true to
form — rose to the challenge. He lunged at me and sunk his
teeth deeply into my arm.

"Oh my God," I thought, "I'm done for." I grabbed hold of

Harry's collar and raced him through the house to the back door. I wasn't sure I could hold him, unlock the door, open it, and put him out. I could tell he had sobered, but I was only just becoming aware of how much terror I felt. With steely determination not to let go of the wild thing, I got the door open and shoved Harry outside. He turned and sat at the door, his ears hanging low, his tail between his legs, and his usually bright eyes looking dim. Large, wet snowflakes swirled around his head and settled to the ground. I looked down at my arm and saw blood seeping through my sleeve.

What had gone wrong to make my dog bite me? I had done what dog trainers and owners had advised me to do. I had mastered the alpha roll whenever Harry didn't listen. I had confronted Harry's increasing belligerence. I withheld food, I gave food, I changed where I gave food. I made him sit, demanded he lie down, and I taught him to place his tennis ball in my hand when we played. I tethered him; I let him go free. I took away his bones when he glared at me, showing his teeth. I had even confronted his growling by grabbing his collar and whisking him away. It was becoming clear that Harry was aggressive, but it seemed that the more I tried to deal with it, the more aggressive he became. I began to think there was more to this than I knew. Maybe there was something wrong with *me*.

Dogs never bite the hand that feeds them, or so I thought. How unnatural was I? I had been looking at Harry's eyes when he growled at me. Was I conveying a threat? Was I sending messages that I was totally unaware of? As a psychotherapist, I was aware of how unconscious messages can be conveyed to others, and I became concerned that there was a whole area of my being I might be unaware of that was being illuminated in stark reality in this human-canine relationship. I really felt like a mother who was unable to breastfeed her own infant. There must be something terribly wrong with me. Something terribly unnatural. For dogs never lie about love, according to the book by Jeffrey

Moussaieff Masson. Everyone knows dogs have an uncanny ability to perceive the intentions of evil people. I was beginning to wonder what this was saying about me.

It hadn't been that long ago that my sister, my nephew, and I had gone to the pound. We saw the dog with no name sitting bolt upright, head held high behind the thick iron bars of doggy prison. A stray found on a street corner; wiry brindle hair with scraggly whiskers and beard. He was underweight with an over-the-top attitude. A street kid in dog form. I loved him the moment I saw him.

On that fateful day that Harry bit me, my sister picked me up at the hospital. My arm now bandaged, we went inside to deal with the little terrorist. Harry was barricaded behind my glass-paned door that separated the living room from the dining room. I could see him lying on his bed. I thought he looked contrite. He roused himself and stared uncomprehendingly through the door at us. He then lay down again in what seemed a state of resignation.

I called the Humane Society to find out what needed to be done. I was told that Harry would be signed over to them to be euthanized. Already I felt the loss of his companionship. The magnificent beast that I was supposed to have rescued was now going to be executed because of me.

The public health officer who came to take Harry away was bald and had most of his fingernails missing. I wondered about him. His name was Joe. A fitting name for someone with an imposing physical appearance, though it belied his gentle soul. Joe informed me I didn't have to sign Harry over immediately. I actually had ten days to consider his fate. I choked back tears with a mixture of relief and fear. If he were euthanized, the situation would be resolved and I wouldn't have to face the fear I felt towards my beloved dog. I felt relieved that the ultimate decision would be delayed. Joe opened the door to the dining room to take Harry away, and I was awash with so much sadness, I could no longer contain my tears.

I wanted to hug Harry and tell him it would be okay — but it probably wasn't going to be. I wanted to change my mind and keep Harry with me, but I was too afraid. Joe was being gentle. He said he is usually rough with aggressive dogs but knew that would upset me. Harry came out of the dining room, at first tentative, then trusting, going for "walkies" with Joe. Joe took him to the van that carried him away for what I thought would be forever. Sob after sob erupted from inside me. The feeling of loss for Harry was triggering the many early losses I had sustained during my life. I knew Harry would be afraid, and I felt so sad believing I had failed him. He would be alone again in a cage with a cold concrete floor at the Humane Society, and I knew how much Harry loved to be free. My dog was going away and all I could imagine was a euthanizing needle in his leg and the life slowly receding from his beautiful eyes.

I called Suzanne, my dog trainer, to tell her what had transpired. Shortly after I had adopted Harry, she advised me that he had aggressive tendencies and suggested I send him to a canine aggression expert. What? My sweet puppy, aggressive? Preposterous! I also believed that I could melt away Harry's stubborn resistance through kind and patient love.

I was now being jarred into a realization that love was not enough for a dog like Harry. He needed something different, something more than I knew how to give. Despite what others were saying about how bad Harry was, I suspected that I was the one who had let him down.

Late that night I had a call from Adam Stone, a canine aggression expert. Suzanne had told him what happened and Adam wanted to talk to me about my options for Harry. He generously offered to take Harry to make sure that he was capable of being rehabilitated — most if not all dogs are, according to Stone. Once Harry was rehabilitated, I could have him back, or Adam would find another home for him. I couldn't believe that Harry was going to have another chance. Nonetheless, I still had mixed emotions. I was terrified of Harry, and I couldn't imagine overcoming my fear. But our life together had been far too short. To think of him being executed was breaking my heart.

There really was no question. If Harry could be saved, he should be. If I couldn't be with Harry, then someone else should be. Harry would go to Adam. Little did I know how profoundly that conversation would alter the course of life for Harry and for me.

Times of Crisis

IT IS OFTEN IN THE darkest times of crisis that we learn most about ourselves. It was in my moment of crisis with Harry that initiated some of the most penetrating learning — so far — in my life. I thought there was something deeply wrong with me to cause my own dog to bite me; after all, I had done nothing but shower my beast with loving kindness. I slowly discovered that the things I thought were wrong weren't. I was asking the wrong questions about myself. Instead of asking what was wrong with me, what was missing in me, I should have been asking what could I develop naturally within me to help me deal with an animal who possessed an inherent mistrust of humans. As I looked back on the past months with Harry, I realized that this wasn't the first time Harry had bitten. It was just the worst bite he had inflicted so far. Harry's early life as a street dog had most probably prepared him for a life of fighting for valuable resources and little to no natural attachment and trust with humans. I had unwittingly engaged in a power struggle with a single-minded beast intent on getting what he wanted, and it led to an escalating miscommunication culminating in me being bitten.

Once I made the decision to give Harry another chance to live, I began a process of learning that changed the way I thought about relationships and myself. Like a kaleidoscope, one small turn and the entire picture transformed, shifting my thinking forever.

My tendency to become awash in self-blame could have kept me from discovering the lesson that was presenting itself, but I chose instead to face it. I didn't know at the time what kind of mental fortitude it would take, nor did I know if I could actually do it, but I wanted to try. I gave up the self-blame and instead engaged in a process of genuine learning. The more I learned about Harry, the more I learned about myself.

The Education of Harry

WHEN HARRY CAME out of the pound for the second time, we immediately drove the three hours to Adam's farm. During the drive, Harry nudged me with his nose from the back seat of the car. I was terrified to look at Harry, even through the rearview mirror, lest I somehow trigger his aggressive behavior once again. We arrived at the farm without incident. For the next seven weeks, I spent three times a week, for hours at a time, in Adam's quaint country kitchen learning about dogs, canine aggression, and communicating with dogs — and with Harry in particular. Adam Stone is fascinating, flamboyant, and — I am fairly certain — part canine himself. Adam never lay blame at my feet for what happened with Harry. He did not contribute to my guilt feelings; he just suggested we move on and help Harry to become a trusted and trusting pet.

The Education of Cindy

INITIALLY I THOUGHT that all I had to do was get over my fear of Harry and continue the training I was learning with Adam. Harry would learn how to "think," make good choices about his actions, and begin to go through life with grace and dignity. Once Harry learned his lessons, everything would be fine. End of story. But, it wasn't to be that easy. Of course, nothing about Harry is ever easy.

It was when I realized that fear was only one of many elements in our relationship that needed to change that I came to understand that I had just as much healing to do as Harry, maybe even more. We needed to heal a damaged trust, create respect for each other, and allow the love to develop naturally from the building we were doing. It was then that the four elements of healing emerged for me as a concept and became the foundation for this book. The four elements of healing:

1. Courage (earth)
2. Trust (water)
3. Respect (air)
4. Love (fire)

I began by learning how to act with courage, while building trust and developing respect. Love grew naturally from there.

Courage

AFTER THE TRAUMA of Harry's bite, fear was ever present in me whenever I was around him. The first night I took Harry home from the farm, I had a friend come to stay overnight. I was afraid to be alone with Harry. It would take every bit of courage I could muster to continue my relationship with him. Courage forms the first element of this book. Learning to act with courage in the face of fear, not in the absence of fear, began my journey to a fuller, richer life.

We are not always aware of how pervasive fear can be in our lives: how we have managed fear, hidden fear, and lived with fear until we discover that we haven't managed fear but fear has managed us. We are not hiding fear, but fear is causing us to hide. We are not living with fear, but being fearful and not living. Learning to live fully is the core theme of this book.

Trust

A DOG BITE IS such a betrayal of trust. For me, the dog bite crisis ranked alongside extra-marital affairs, friendship betrayals, and, the worst of them all, lies and deceits of the soul. The road to building trust between Harry and me required some learning, some patience, and something that I had not anticipated: I had to learn how to trust myself. I had grown used to ignoring my intuition and substituting the advice of others for my own common sense. Though I had to trust that what Adam was teaching would eventually work with Harry, his teaching possessed a rock-solid foundation of natural common sense. The teaching resonated with what I already knew about parenting.

I learned to trust that I could deal with difficulties and know what to do. I learned to trust my judgment and myself. When the elements of healing are employed in life, the subtleties of knowing when to let go, of trusting yourself to know when to stay in a relationship and when to let go, and remaining aware of signs of trouble becomes instinctive.

Respect

I DISCOVERED I had confused generous and indiscriminate giving as a means to create respect with generous and discriminate giving to build authentic respect. I allowed Harry to take advantage of me, to manipulate me, and to usurp my position. Partly because I didn't have the knowledge — that I later gained — to understand the needs of my wilful canine, but mostly because I didn't possess enough self-respect. It was a journey of self-discovery. An early dog lesson, in hindsight, highlights this. A place in the house is reserved for your dog as a boundary. You send the dog to his boundary place whenever you want peace of mind, a quiet dinner without the watchful eye of a drooling animal, or to read without being pawed. I never felt comfortable with this lesson. It felt unfair for me to ask Harry to leave my space for what I perceived as no good reason.

Now I understand all the little ways I led Harry to believe that I didn't deserve any respect: I never asked for any. Harry was quite willing to eat my food, enjoy my affection, and bask in the warmth of my shelter, but as far as respecting me, I had given him no reason to. Harry was certainly teaching me how he wanted to be treated, but I was not teaching him how I wanted to be treated. In Harry's distinctive style, he taught me self-respect through example.

Love

SOME PEOPLE HAVE dogs to work for them; some have dogs for security; I wanted a dog to love. I wanted to love a dog, and I wanted my dog to love me back. Some dogs, like some people, just take a little longer to develop the bonds that bring about a deep and abiding love. Harry had lots of love to give but without the foundation work of our relationship — building trust and respect — the love was not always forthcoming. We often succumb to power struggles because of fear, lack of trust, and little respect. Love doesn't grow or build in an atmosphere of suspicion. The expectation for love to be immediate, rich, and fulfilling is an attitude conditioned by the media and supported by our hopes and dreams. Once again I was learning lessons, this one about love and relationships, and I was learning from a dog!

The Four Elements of Healing: How to Use This Book

THE FOUR ELEMENTS OF healing forms the basis of what I learned from Harry and how that learning can help others heal their relationships with friends, family, partners, and themselves. Each element will be developed fully in the subsequent

chapters. It is not a matter of healing yourself first and your relationships with others will naturally and effortlessly follow suit. If
only life were that easy! If we focus on healing ourselves in the
absence of healing the way we relate to others, we risk becoming
too self-involved and too isolated to make the most of Harry's lessons. It is when we take the chance to be involved with others that
we can best learn how we relate and what that might say about
ourselves. We look at the place of contact between people to
observe ourselves relating.

When we become sensitized to the patterns in our life, the
discovery of our lessons begins. We need to look for patterns in
our friendships, our family relationships, and our love relationships. We need to look for patterns in our disappointments, our
resentments, and in what makes us happy. We also need to look
for the patterns in what we complain about in order to discover
our hidden (or in some cases not so hidden but definitely
ignored) lessons.

Steps to Using the Four Elements of Healing

1. Be courageous:
   - Identify an issue — be honest with yourself.
   - Acquire awareness of the issue and how it affects your life.
2. Be trusting and trustable:
   - Bridge any knowledge gaps that keep you from being fully effective.
   - Work at developing trust in yourself and with others through practice.
3. Be respectful and self-respecting:
   - Develop options to automatic responses. (Exercise your right to free choice!)
   - Pay attention to how you treat others and how you allow others to treat you.

4. Be loving and lovable:
   - Learn to recognize critical inner voices and identify them as such.
5. Begin to see yourself and others more clearly.
   - Stay open to possibilities.

The four elements of healing represents a powerful model when used to develop self-awareness and to create possibilities for new and ever-more satisfying ways of being.

The dramatic incident with Harry led me to more genuinely respect myself, and this naturally led to my having greater respect for others. Facing the fear that I felt towards Harry helped me discover the power of courage. Building trust and observing the ways that trust developed gave me a deeper insight into the nature of trust than I had previously. I began to see trust as something other than a fixed sense of what someone else was doing or not doing. It became a gauge of how I was being in a relationship. How open I was, how trusting I was, how trustable I was, and how aware I was. Love became something that was continually evolving, growing, and deepening. It became something that couldn't be taken for granted. I mapped the learning from Harry onto other situations in my own life, my friends' lives, and those of my families and clients.

The Zen Master

HARRY IS A teacher. A teacher in a form that I did not want, with lessons in a form that I definitely did not want. He is a Zen master in their delivery. I don't get words to grapple with intellectually. Instead, I get an action from Harry, an action that seems to hold enormous weight of meaning for him. Harry constantly questions my lack of clear intention, constantly demands I reflect upon myself, and constantly pushes me to my limits. If I am the least bit ambivalent about a directive, Harry takes advantage. If I pay attention to my insecurities, Harry supersedes me. If

I intellectualize what should be a common gut response, Harry gets confused and strikes out on his own.

The dog as teacher has been alluded to for centuries. Franz Kafka, in *Investigations of a Dog*, writes, "All knowledge, the totality of all questions and answers, is contained in the dog." Raphael, a character from a Charles Kingsley play, describes the deeply spiritual experience of learning from a dog: "I took her, my dog, for my teacher and obeyed her, for she was wiser than I, and she led me back, poor dumb beast, like a God-sent, and God-obeying angel, to human nature, to mercy, to self-sacrifice, to belief, to worship, to pure and wedded love."

In "Murphy's Romance," an article that appeared in *O, The Oprah Magazine*, columnist Craig Wilson writes, "My life changed dramatically ten years ago. I didn't get married, or divorced, didn't survive a life-threatening disease, didn't have a religious experience—then again, maybe I did. I got a dog."

A dog as a religious experience? A dog as a guru? A dog the vessel of vital knowledge? You might be thinking that those of us who have lost our hearts to our dogs might have also lost our minds. I don't think so. Dogs have a unique way of being in our world. They live fully in the moment, without pretense or masks. In fact, it seems that dogs are incapable of being deceitful about their feelings. If they are injured, they whimper. If they are sick, they lie down. If they are hungry, they eat. If they are angry and frustrated, they will bite. Humans, on the other hand, if they feel unwell will tend to minimize it, cover it up, or "put a smile" on their faces. That is what makes dogs such incredible teachers for humans who have learned, in the service of civility, tiny deceits of the heart and soul. Robert Caras writes in *A Dog is Listening*, "A dog is utterly sincere. It cannot pretend."

Building Bonds

OFTEN WHEN WE are faced with difficult situations that frighten or challenge us, we either remain with our first instinct — to ascribe blame (to ourselves or to someone or something else) — or we don't stay with the situation sufficiently to gain the learning necessary. It takes time to learn. We live in a society where we believe in quick fixes and immediate results, and we no longer take the time to truly learn. Georgia O'Keefe, a painter of enormous and voluptuous flowers said, "Nobody sees a flower, really — it is so small — we haven't the time and to see takes time, like to have a friend takes time." Like to build a bond with a dog takes time. To build a bond with a street dog of an unknown past can take even more time. I love O'Keefe's quote because it epitomizes what we all have come to expect in our world: instant bonds and instant learning, and if things aren't progressing rapidly enough, we think something is wrong.

Before the biting crisis, I was engaged in the problem of trying to train Harry, of teaching Harry how to respond to me, to respect me, but I had no prior experience and no understanding of the kind of dog I was dealing with. I didn't feel I was getting anywhere, and when the animal urchin would flip his furry finger at me and run in the other direction when I wanted him to run to me, I got frustrated. I was willing to trade the slow building of respect with Harry for the speedy but illusory closeness that comes with using food bribes and lures to gain compliance.

I would see people at the beach with their pockets and waist pouches bulging with countless varieties of doggy treats. Everyone was extremely generous in doling out biscuits to great hordes of dogs sitting pretty waiting for their treats. None could sit so pretty and take the biscuits so gently as Harry. He would cock his head to one side and look deeply and earnestly into the eyes of the treat-giver, knowing a second cookie would be coaxed from the furless being. The siren call of using doggie treats lured me in an effort to forge the closeness with Harry that I so desired yet felt eluded me.

Over a short period, Harry became a cookie monster and his behavior rapidly deteriorated. The relationship I had been trying to build with Harry became a trading game: "Give me a cookie and I will come to you." "Na, na, na, na, na ... catch me if you can!" He would deke away at the last minute. I could almost hear him say, "If you need a cookie to get me to come close to you, you don't deserve me as a dog." That thought was certainly a projection of my own sense of inadequacy, but if Harry could think a complex thought like that — and I am not so sure he cannot — he definitely would have thought it.

The Blaming Game

WHEN WE LOOK for causes outside ourselves during times of crisis, our tendency is to be reactive. We become victims rather than approaching the crisis as an opportunity to learn about ourselves. Often, we fall into the pattern of blame when problems arise in our relationships; the situation immediately becomes reactive. For example, one member of a couple might feel unsupported by the other. If we give into blaming the other for not sufficiently understanding our needs, we miss the opportunity to learn the wider, deeper lessons. What have I communicated to my partner? What has he or she communicated to me? Do I support my partner in his or her time of need? Do I allow someone to support me in mine? There are countless issues that evolve over time in a relationship, and blame most often obscures what it really going on and what really needs to happen in order to facilitate the fulfillment of two individuals engaged in that relationship.

Another example of a prime situation for learning is those instances when someone feels a friend or a boss does not value him or her. All too often, instead of looking at ways to change the situation, the person walks away, blaming the friend or boss for any number of insensitivities or failings. When a person walks away from a situation before taking the time to evaluate the best possible course of action, it is most often a knee-jerk reaction that justifies the self and avoids taking responsibility, ultimately missing the opportunity for learning a lesson inherent in the situation.

But, don't worry, the lessons will arise once again to see if you are awake the next time! Some people need a little hint to tell them that something needs attention. Others need a little prodding, some a little pushing, and then there are those like me, who need to be bitten to be awakened.

Always Another Opportunity

WHEN MY PRECOCIOUS stepdaughter was young, she used to come to me and present me with very difficult questions. I discovered that, if I didn't know the answers or she wasn't satisfied with my feeble attempts, the opportunity for a different response would offer itself yet again if I waited long enough. Sarah was the kind of child who never lets you off the hook with an inadequate response, a half-hearted answer, or an incomplete solution. She was a lesson in providing plenty of opportunities to solve issues — luckily for me, since as a writer I am more likely to ponder an issue for several days. I'm not one of those quick-witted women you see in the movies who always have brilliant and instant quips that impress everyone. For Sarah, once an issue was resolved to her satisfaction, it never came up again.

Sarah is no less tenacious as a young adult, though her questions are more profound. It isn't surprising to me that she spent her first year in university studying philosophy and her second studying cultural anthropology. Sarah wanted the questions that burned in her soul to be answered by philosophy, found it too wedded to Western thought for her taste, so went on to look for answers in other cultures.

Holes in Our Being

AS A PSYCHOTHERAPIST and an executive coach, I have had ample opportunity to help others engage in their discovery of personal life lessons hiding within crises. One example that comes to mind is an incredibly bright man who constantly doubted his abilities despite being awarded a scholarship and earning a graduate degree in business from Harvard University. He was a business consultant with one of the most prestigious consulting firms in the world and was asked to participate in countless forums with other experts. He constantly found ways to denigrate his successes and held himself back from opportunities in case he was revealed as being "deficient" intellectually. The evidence abounded that he was an extraordinary individual, but he refused to believe it, until he came to me and confessed his sense of inferiority.

He came in a crisis of confidence that was beginning to debilitate him and would likely eventually effect the great work he was doing. We explored the possibility that he might be inferior (and with his inferior intellect had merely fooled all the really intelligent people). We rigorously looked for evidence that would prove his inadequacies. We found none. We engaged in a process that allowed him to see himself — not through his own overly critical eyes — but through the eyes of someone with clear sight. He stopped listening to empty praise that served only to support his feeling that he was a fraud and began to look and listen for the substance of what he was doing. It gave him clarity to see what he was doing well and what he needed to improve. Today he travels the world and is one of the company's top consultants. He now works with confidence and no longer feels he is an intellectual impostor.

Like a shoemaker who has holes in his own shoes, I had some holes in my being that I had — so I thought — successfully dealt with or at least managed. I hadn't expected to have such difficult problems with my dog. I expected to have a loyal, loving companion, woman's best friend kind of thing without too much hard work. I was prepared to train Harry, but I hadn't bargained for such stubborn, aggressive resistance. I certainly hadn't imagined that I would learn my life lesson so viscerally.

Discovering Our Lessons

IT IS IN THE ordinary stuff of daily life that we often find our lessons that are there for the learning. Regrettably, I had missed many opportunities in my life to learn the lessons of healing which I eventually came to learn from Harry. I could have learned them from teachers, from my relationships, from my stepdaughter, my sister, my family, my friends, and I could go on ad nauseam about the opportunities I allowed to pass me by. Harry's teeth made an impression on me — literally. I shall bear the scar for the rest of my life. Perhaps if I had learned the lesson in other situations, I wouldn't have needed such a shocking method of delivery. But the learning has been invaluable. When I think that I could have easily overlooked this opportunity for learning by having Harry euthanized or giving him away, I shudder. There is a story that I find relevant that goes something like this:

There was a man who was a sole survivor of a shipwreck and he clung tenaciously to a piece of wood while bobbing like a cork in the vast ocean. A fishing boat came by, saw the man, and got close enough to pick him up. They threw out lines to him and the man said, "Oh, don't worry, I'm waiting for God to save me." The fishing boat went off without him. A day later, an ocean liner happened to go by and notice him. It sent out a life-saving raft and when it approached the man, he said, "Oh, don't worry, I'm waiting for God to save me." So the raft went back to the ocean liner and it went on its way. On the third day, a helicopter flew overhead and noticed the man bobbing in the ocean. It hovered overhead and sent down a lifeline. The man said, "Oh, don't worry, I'm waiting for God to save me." They pulled up the lifeline and flew off, leaving the man behind. On the fourth day, the man was still bobbing in the ocean, and he said to God, "I've been waiting for four days now for you to save me. I've waited with patience and with absolute faith, I hope you come to save me soon." God answered, "I've already sent you a fishing boat, an ocean liner, and a helicopter. When are you going to start taking my help?"

Like the man in the boat, I needed to be open to what was being offered, instead of thinking I already knew what was coming my way. It is this presumption that can steer us away from valuable learning opportunities. Whenever we think we know what lesson it is we need to learn, life has a way of providing us with the one we *really* need to learn.

At times I would love to miss those opportunities, particularly when they hurt. However, it seems when I miss or dismiss an opportunity for learning, the following one becomes more dramatic.

Problem Dogs

EACH YEAR IN the United States there are 4.7 million dog bites, 800,000 of them serious. Dog bites are the leading cause of facial disfigurement in children in North America. Dr. Nicholas Dodman, an expert on the behavioral problems of dogs, asserts that unwelcome behavior in dogs is the leading cause of canine deaths, not disease, nor overpopulation, nor indiscriminate breeding. In Elizabeth Marshall Thomas's book The Social Lives of Dogs, she quotes Dodman describing the usual fate of problem dogs: "People acquire a dog, don't understand it, can't train it, get fed up and take it to the local humane society where they offer it for adoption, hoping to pass on the problem to somebody else. But nobody wants a problem dog, and the shelter is already overrun with similar dogs."

I have come to believe that problem dogs are not just a training issue. The issue is also about people finding out who they are being in their relationships with themselves, with their pets, and with others. It is developing a constant awareness of what is being created in the relationship at any given moment. Starting a relationship with a dog is a serious commitment, and as in relationships with humans, you can't always rely on them to act the way you want them to. Sometimes relationships take work, usually when you expect that they won't.

Only a few weeks ago, a young girl was viciously attacked by two pitbull-Akita crossmixed dogs. Pitbulls are known for their tenacious grips, and Akitas are fighting dogs. The combination of the two is formidable. The girl was left traumatized and has sustained permanent physical damage to her face and ear. The dogs' owner lived in an apartment in a busy section of a busy city. The girl was walking past the woman and her two dogs on the sidewalk. The woman was unable to hold the dogs, and first one attacked, the second joining in. The first dog had a muzzle order from a previous attack. The owner said she had not yet fastened the muzzle on her dog before the walk. Why not is a mystery, but what is more of a mystery is why she didn't look for a way to heal her dog. I suspect there would have been some very different healing going on if the woman had heeded the signs her dogs were giving. This situation is tragic and appalling, and it might have been avoided.

There are ways to teach aggressive dogs to behave responsibly and appropriately. I have learned that obedience training is not one of them, certainly not in the case of Harry. Obedience can mask the problem of aggression but it does not necessarily solve the problem. Obedience seeks to control a dog, whereas behavior training seeks to teach the dog to manage its own behavior. Canine aggression exists in environments where it is unwittingly reinforced, ignored, denied — or worse — not only supported but encouraged (for example, dogs used for personal security). It takes some self-deception to maintain an environment where there is a potentially dangerous problem that is not being addressed. We get the wake-up calls daily! We need to pay attention to them and deal with them.

Rarely do things happen without signs and signals beforehand. Sometimes the signs are so subtle it is understandable that they are missed. Sometimes hindsight puts the signals in such bold relief we really wonder about ourselves and how we could have so easily missed them. I participate in an ongoing canine aggression clinic run by Adam Stone. The class is filled with people learning how to deal with their aggressive dogs. New people invariably come to class and downplay their dogs' aggression. "Oh no! Heavens no! My little Suzy never bit anyone before." Adam pushes a little more, "Are you sure, because this dog is showing signs of acting very unpleasant around people!" The owner answers, "Well, she bit a dog once, but the dog was playing with her roughly so he deserved it ... (pause) well, she did growl at the child next door ... (pause) and she did bite the vet, but that was when he was checking her ears ...." It often takes a few prompts, but once owners begin to think about it, they find numerous incidents of transgressions towards others by their cute little wolves-in-sheep's-clothing.

Today when I walk Harry, people come up to me and tell me what an adorable, wonderful, well-behaved dog I have. I can't help but swell with pride, but I do take a deep breath and reveal that it wasn't always this way. By being open about my experience, I am discovering that there are many dogs that have problems their humans are either too embarrassed about or too perplexed about to know what to do. These are good, loving people revealing their stories, often for the first time.

People have confided in me that their dogs have bitten letter carriers, their children, visiting children, or the owners themselves. It is as though the problem dog has to be kept a well-guarded secret, like we once kept the secret of child abuse and sexual abuse. Once the secret comes out of the closet, more and more people can be helped, more and more dogs can not only be saved from execution but given fuller, richer lives. As humans, by pushing through what seems to be an impossible situation, we can learn what it takes to create committed relationships with equality and mutuality, and enjoy the fulfillment that comes from being a whole person. Rather than maintaining the secret, we need to be open to the learning.

I have a friend, Eileen, whose large yellow Labrador ruled her entire home. Yellow Labs are known for their gentle temperaments and easy dispositions. Sasha was a bit different. The dog bit one of her children, a man delivering handbills, and even Eileen, though she remains convinced it was a mistake. If Eileen was on the telephone, Sasha would bark incessantly and nip at her feet until she hung up. The dog reluctantly allowed Eileen to go to bed in the evenings, and if she moved in her sleep during the night, the dog would leap up and growl menacingly. This type of behavior is not as uncommon as we might think.

Another friend, Allison, had a cute small dog that ruled the roost and one day bit her son when he tried to pat her. The dog was then given away to a childless couple. When that didn't work, the dog was sent to meet her maker.

When people have problem dogs, they learn how to construct a world that mostly keeps the dog confined or otherwise out of trouble. I preferred to find a way to give Harry the gift of good choices so that he can be free, and people can come to my house or office even if they don't like dogs. I took the opportunity that Harry gave me to dig deep into my soul to discover the places that I needed to heal in order to help Harry heal. Harry has learned how to conduct himself responsibly in social situations. He goes to my local bookstores with me, he is invited to friends' houses, and he will wait untied in front of stores for me without kicking up a fuss. There are still many things he has to learn, but we now have mutuality in our relationship that allows us to navigate difficult situations.

Dogs and Humans

DOGS SHARE 99 percent of their genes with wolves. And wolves share 75 percent of their genes with humans. It is no wonder that wolves and dogs have fascinated us for centuries. Jeffrey Moussaieff Masson, in his book *The Emperor's Embrace*, talks lovingly about the intimacy shared in the life of dogs and humans over thousands of years, suggesting that perhaps it was not necessarily humans who chose the wolf to domesticate but the wolf that chose us. Moussaieff Masson observes the ways dogs and humans attempt to learn from each other. I doubt that he is talking about our teaching dogs to sit, stay, lie down, come, and heel. There had to be deeper learning going on for our dog and human relationships to have become so profound.

Teaching a dog to sit, stay, lie down, come, and heel has to be the least fulfilling aspect of creating a relationship with a dog. Through my training with Adam, I learned that dogs have a much greater capacity for thinking and learning than obedience commands allow for; obedience training restricts the free expression of who the dogs are capable of becoming. Charles Eisenmann, the owner and trainer of the Littlest Hobo, did not train his dogs using obedience drills. He communicated with his dogs by enlisting their thinking when teaching them to perform.

Obedience training requires a dog to act in accordance with our supreme authority as the owner of the inferior animal, which must remain under our control and do our bidding. The training I learned from Adam for Harry — once his aggression was dealt with — was to engage Harry's mind and allow him to make mistakes in order to learn from them. The training centered on the emotional bonding in the relationship between human and dog. Harry would work out his "Harry-ness" and I would learn that I could trust him to make good decisions for himself, and in that environment, love would grow.

On the first day of this training with Adam, Harry bolted from my side, engaged a rottweiler — sitting comfortably on his own porch — to play, then ran into the people's house. Adam's response was, "Great!" I was appalled at Harry's behavior. Adam explained to me that Harry does not feel oppressed by me and so will explore his personal boundaries. He will eventually sort out how to behave because he has learned what is right and has strengthened his bond with me. My obedience mindset was that I should have Harry walk beside me in a dignified manner and not give another dog a second look. Adam explained that when Harry behaves with dignity, I would know that Harry was behaving well because he knew it was the right thing to do, not because I controlled his behavior through negative or positive reinforcements. Of course, you must be at a point in your relationship with your dog where the cornerstones of trust, respect, and love are well grounded and the aggression is clearly gone in order to do this kind of "guru" training. The basic concept is to not *have* to control your dog; your dog manages his own good behavior. This idea appeals to me far more than having to spend the rest of my life governing another being's behavior, even if that being is a dog.

The Journey Begins

NOTHING HAS FORCED me to become more clear, more authentic, more congruous as a person than working with Harry. He just won't accept anything less of me. I cannot act in any way other than authentically. I cannot fool him or dazzle him with my facility with words. I just have to be. I had to learn the lessons this time or learn to live without my beloved canine companion. I couldn't bear the thought of executing Harry. This was my crisis. I had thought that something was inherently wrong with me, that I was unable to create the relationship I desired with Harry. But what I discovered was that there was nothing wrong with me. I discovered I was just hiding. I needed to look deep into the half-born reservoirs of my self to find who I really was. I needed to stop confronting Harry and start confronting myself. I needed to go with courage, trust myself, respect myself, and love from wholeness.

I happened to get a dog for my teacher. Fact is, I couldn't have found anyone better. Harry uses no words with which to obfuscate intent. He is pure emotion. He is pure action. He is pure being in the moment. He is my constant reminder of the absurdity of life. The four elements of healing — courage, trust, respect, and love — transformed my life. With the willingness to look deeply and openly into your own life, a transformation can and will take place. This is a book about becoming. This is a book about what Harry taught me.

Harry on Courage:
Fear Rules If You Let It!

Believe in yourself. You gain strength, courage,
and confidence by every experience in which you
stop to look fear in the face. You must do that
which you think you cannot do.

— ELEANOR ROOSEVELT

Harry's wild nature half fascinated, half repelled me. The feral beast masquerading as a Disney dog now terri-fied me. There was no denying it; I was feeling abject fear. I could not erase the image of Harry baring his teeth, lunging at me, and sinking his teeth deep into my arm. I wasn't sure I would ever get over it.

Being forced to deal with the chastening fear for my physical safety, I learned more about fear than I had ever wished to learn from my incidental guru. The situation flipped open the lid on how I contain fear, how I do and do not deal with physical fears, and how I avoid challenging myself in life because of emotional fears. This brought me closer to understanding fear than any other experience in my life. Because the situation was ongoing,

I had ample opportunity to analyze my reactions. I wasn't all that happy with what I discovered. I deal with both physical and emotional threats weakly and I am easily intimidated. When dealing with emotional fears, I often give up, leaving myself unfulfilled in life.

Two Sides of a Coin: Courage and Fear

IT IS ALMOST impossible to talk about courage without talking also about fear. They are two sides of a coin. Courage moves into actuality precisely because of the existence of fear. They are intrinsically linked. When someone acts with courage it is because he or she has acted in the face of fear. If no fear is present, the need for courage doesn't exist. The amount of courage needed to act is proportional to the amount of fear experienced.

Part of healing is to understand our own fears, their purpose in our lives, and how our fears might keep us from becoming fulfilled. There is the fear that fueled Harry's aggression and the fear I experienced knowing what terrible feats Harry was capable of. Then there is the insidious fear that was keeping me from achieving my aspirations — my fear of discovering that I wasn't capable of achieving them. This fear is not uncommon, and it can rule our lives if we allow it. Learning to deal with fear is a pathway to freedom. Ralph Ellison, author of *The Invisible Man*, once said, "When I discover who I am, I will be free." I believe that knowing our personal relationship to fear is a significant step to knowing who we are and who we are being in our world.

When I first began writing this chapter, it was all about fear, because fear was all I felt. It was about finding fear, feeling fear, and understanding fear, but it wasn't about healing fear. At that time it never occurred to me that there could be a healing. My fear was visceral and it seemed that it might never leave me. I was so ensconced in fear that I couldn't imagine anything different. I would handle my fear in the only way I knew how — by coping.

The incidental guru would have a different lesson in mind for me. This time coping with fear would not be enough. I would have to heal. I would have to find my own source of courage.

Tactical Responses

THE PHYSICAL THREAT of Harry put me in touch with the rather limited methods I use to deal with physical threat. Most humans and animals have an array of tactics to draw on in the face of threat — some very effective, others less so. Some run away, some fight back, some use cunning or intelligence to outwit the aggressor, some use diplomacy, and some just plain hide. In the face of threat possums play dead, deer freeze or take flight, chameleons change their colors, and lizards literally lose their tails.

You can observe multiple tactics used in the canine world to deal with a physical threat. Some dogs run away. Some raise their hackles, apparently to appear larger and more imposing, which can either stop a fight or present an outright challenge to the aggressor. Some dogs curl their lips, show their teeth, and growl. Some jump right in and attack the aggressor in a direct confrontation. Some use a variety of posturing tactics to avoid fighting. Still others become submissive, rolling onto their backs and licking their lips so they don't appear threatening, thereby avoiding the fight. Submission doesn't always work as a tactic, though. It can actually provoke a fight in certain kinds of aggressive dogs that cannot tolerate submission or that have not learned to adequately distinguish hostile or friendly intentions.

I have often been a deer-in-the-headlight kind of woman: frozen solid, no response, no mental activity of any kind, just a total abdication of body and mind. My limited array of tactics depends on the context. I have at times "rolled over" in the hope that I wouldn't appear a threat. I have solicited the support of someone I think is better than I. In my vain attempts to be powerful, I have engaged in battles over things I am totally unskilled in, thereby generating a power struggle. I have not been too effective overall. I have spun my tactics as diplomatic skill, but when I really look at myself through the eyes of a dominant dog, I see that I was not diplomatic — I was weak. I am intelligent enough to deceive myself by rationalizing my actions in a variety of ways. This was a critical reason that my dog came to be my incidental guru. Harry is capable of uncovering my self-deceptions and forcing me to deal with them. I have no diplomatic skill; I am a coward! This realization really rocked me. It is not how I wanted to be.

Through Harry's teaching I came to realize that I don't like dealing with problems. I just want them to go away. But the problem of my biting dog was huge and would not go away unless I sent Harry away. I wanted to stick my head in the sand like an ostrich and wish for someone else to deal with my problem. But this time I couldn't act helpless or Harry would forever disrespect me. As much as I don't like to admit it, I had a *weak* response to fear.

This doesn't mean that responding powerfully to physical fear requires engaging directly in a physical battle. Tried that. It resulted in disaster. Harry's teeth are much larger than mine are. I had been acting on the suggestion from many dog owners and some dog trainers to use the alpha roll to deal with a dominant dog. I became adept at flipping my seventy-five-pound male over on his back when he did something he wasn't supposed to, like chase a bicyclist or a jogger. It was after only a few weeks of that treatment combined with food lures that I ended up bitten. In Elizabeth Marshall Thomas's book *The Social Lives of Dogs*, she tells a similar story about a man who read the writings of Konrad Lorenz, the famous Austrian naturalist who advised people to shake their dogs by the scruff of their necks for discipline. The idea is that the dog will feel that a much larger dog is in charge. The man did this with his husky and as a result was bitten. He did not try it again.

Run Away! Run Away!

I COULD NO LONGER run away when confronted. I couldn't be a coward. I had to become courageous. Easier said than done. It would have been perfectly understandable and socially acceptable to give up an aggressive dog or to have had him executed. Everyone thought I was crazy to even attempt Harry's rehabilitation. "Why bother wasting your time on an aggressive dog?" people asked. "There are lots of great dogs you can get. How about a nice, gentle golden retriever, or a spaniel?" But I just knew, intuitively, that there was something here for me to learn. I had adopted Harry and I felt a responsibility to see through what I had started. I hoped there might be a way to teach Harry how to heal and become a socially responsible dog; I hadn't counted on learning and healing so much of myself in the process.

Though I wanted to give up and put the responsibility of train-ing on someone else, that would not be the answer for me. I had to find a source of courage to face my fear of physical harm. More insidious would be facing my deepest and most hidden fear — that I was inherently unworthy and ultimately unable to commu-nicate with my dog. I believed that to communicate with an ani-mal was the ultimate measure of human authenticity.

My confidence in the way I perceived the world and myself was severely shaken. All the courage I had used until this point in my life became meaningless to me. I had always suspected courage was something I didn't possess. Now I was sure of it. Of course, I hadn't truly understood that communicating with an aggressive dog required a certain kind of skill. That those skills coincided with what I believed was fundamentally missing in me was serendipitous for my education as a human being.

Conjuring courage when you believe that it is a quality born only in others but not in yourself is difficult if not impossible. Courage is something, I had come to believe, people other than me possessed. I felt that when I had required courage, I had fallen far short of the mark I had set for myself. I had witnessed courage in others in both large and small ways. I admire my sister, Wendy, for her ability to stand up to others. She is a tigress when someone she loves is threatened, and she is equally adept at standing up for herself.

Wendy told me that when she was a child the biggest bully at school, Lillian, used to chase her home every day to beat her up. I was younger and at home with my mother. I remember days Wendy would come in after school crying, bruised, and bloodied. Wendy would complain to our mother, who, unbeknownst to us, was ill with cancer and slowly dying. My mother would say, "Run faster, if you don't want to get beaten up." Every day Wendy would run a bit faster, and she would get beaten up a little closer to home. Finally one day she reached the far end of our yard, turned around, and slugged Lillian. Wendy said she decided at that moment she would never be bullied again, and she would never stand by to watch someone else be bullied. By the time I began school, my older sister, already a known tigress, made me safe. I was never challenged while she was around.

That wasn't the only story from childhood of my sister the hero. Wendy told me that the farmer, old Mr. Hannah, who owned the apple orchard bordering the back of our property, kidnapped the children who sneaked into his fields to take apples. She said he put them in his basement and fed them bread and water. She told me that at night when I was asleep she would go and free the children. I believed that story for quite a while. Perhaps this story was the precursor to my sister finding her own source of courage. Stories are how we learn, how we define ourselves, our families, and our communities. Stories are how we create ourselves and our worlds, understand them, and live them. Around the world people use stories to teach deep spiritual and life lessons.

Sometimes our lives change and we forget we no longer have to live by the old stories. Where once we may have been skinny, awkward, and pock-marked adolescents, now we might be tall, slender, and elegant adults. We may carry into adulthood the memory of not understanding something as a child, using the incident to define ourselves as insufficiently intelligent. We sometimes hang onto our fear rather than create and adopt a new story about ourselves as courageous. Our old stories become safe and comfortable, like well-worn shoes, even if they limit us. Creating new stories can be invigorating and exciting, leading us into new experiences, and helping us deal effectively with challenges.

If we consciously create a new story for ourselves, the words must be carefully chosen because the way we use our words can often free us from constraints or further imprison us. According to the psychologists Virginia Sapir and Benjamin Whorf, language constructs reality. If we say we are shy, we are more likely to behave shyly. If we declare we are fearful, we are more likely to behave with fear and less likely with courage. If we say we are confident, we exude confidence. The more we say something, the more we tend to behave that way, like the child whose mother repeatedly says, "You are bad! You are stupid!" comes to believe this and behaves accordingly.

In a different dramatic display of physical courage, my tae kwon-do teacher, Marvin Persaud, a third-degree black belt, ran into a burning building not once but three times to save the lives of four children. What would I have done faced with a similar challenge? What would I have done if I lived in the American South in the 1960s, or Germany in the 1940s, in South Africa or Bosnia? Would I have succumbed to the pressure of the place or time or would I have had the courage of my convictions?

If you ask Marvin what compelled him to risk his life to save three children, he would answer easily. He would say the need to save the children compelled him. Marvin's actions were born out of love and respect for human life. He probably didn't even feel his own fear as he entered the burning house. His self-awareness melted away and he lost concern for his own self as his attention became focused on another. Fear became irrelevant to him when someone else was in need. Marvin committed a selfless act.

I had been in the presence of courageous people, yet I felt my own source of courage was somehow lacking. Harry made sure that I would not be allowed to skip over this significant experience. I would have to learn about fear and courage from the inside out. Courage would no longer be a quality I would admire from a distance; it would become something inherent that I could call on when needed.

The Physiology of Fear

WHETHER THE THREAT is physical, such as being attacked by a saber-toothed tiger (or vicious dog) or emotional, such as the telephone ringing in the middle of the night, our sensation of fear is a physiological response, firing up hormones that are then let loose in the body. As a species, we now have fewer reasons for physical fears than we did at an earlier time in our development, when survival was more a matter of "eat or be eaten." Our society has developed to the point where we are unlikely to be facing down our next meal with just a spear and our own physical faculties. Then, fear was a visceral reaction that prompted us into life-saving action. Our emotions have not caught up to these developments, and so when we feel fear, a host of physical responses flood our bodies with hormones.

We may simply be going to meet the in-laws, but our bodies react as though we were meeting face to face with ravenous man-eating lions. "Negative emotions like fear make high metabolic demands on our bodies, creating a state of intense physiological arousal," describes author Arthur Ciaramicoli. Because the situation doesn't require a physical response like fight or flee but requires us instead to calmly extend our hand in friendship and shake the hand of our threat — in this case, our in-laws — our physiology is stuck having to deal with these chemical responses.

It may be that the frequency of such chemical floods contributes to the high numbers of panic and anxiety disorders today. Often, when we need to react physically in the face of a genuine physical threat, we are insufficiently in touch with our instinctual responses to be effective.

Though we are still learning the intricacies of the brain, it is thought that the neocortex, which wraps around the amygdala, brings conscious thought and the ability to determine reactions and behavior. Neocortically driven mammals possess the capability for the more complex and nuanced emotions of sympathy, stress, amusement, anxiety, and annoyance rather than for the amygdala-determined heightened emotions of raw fear, anger, sadness, and joy. It is the neocortex that allows us to gain freedom from our habitual responses by determining first through conscious decision how we are going to respond to a given situation. So it is believed to be the neocortex that we are engaging in our dogs when we teach them how to self-correct, how to maintain self-control, and how to determine appropriate behavior according to the rules of the human packs.

In *The Power of Empathy*, Arthur Ciaramicoli mentions a revealing and disturbing study of monkeys raised in the wild. Researchers captured wild monkeys, severed the connections between the neocortex and the amygdala, then returned the monkeys to the wild. The monkeys were no longer capable of discerning other monkeys' hostile or friendly intent. The monkeys could not "reason" what the other monkeys' intentions were and instead reacted with anger and fear. The monkeys did not engage with their former friends and family. The qualities of loyalty, devotion, and kindness seemed to be lost forever to the damaged monkeys. This study clearly illustrates the value to animals of knowing how to think, how to engage in making choices about what is friendly, what is not, and how to react and how not to react.

If we can teach a dog how to engage its neocortex over its amygdala in thinking before reacting, then surely people should be able to gain ascendancy over the reactions driven by the amygdala. In humans, it is not about repressing emotions but about choosing how we are going to react in given situations. Courage may be our neocortex overriding our amygdala. The Dalai Lama is very clear on this subject. In his book *Ancient Wisdom, Modern World: Ethics for the New Millennium*, he says, "Restraining our response to negative thoughts and emotions is not just a matter of suppressing them: insight into their destructive nature is crucial."

Though today's society has changed dramatically, there are still physically threatening situations. Ask any child about the local bully in the schoolyard and hanging around the neighborhood. Racial and religious hatreds threaten the sense of physical security for many people and there are still families where violence exacts its ugly toll on its members. These are escalating issues of fear and aggression that as a society we need to think about and address more actively. We need to summon the courage to understand the fears driving many of these hurtful and violent reactions. Becoming sensitive to these social issues leads to deeper compassion for all beings with whom we are intrinsically connected to and with whom we share our planet. We need to find the courage to look deeper within ourselves to build a better, more compassionate, and more tolerant world.

The Importance of Fear

"YOU HAVE TO BE afraid so you respect what you are doing," said Michelle Yeoh, accepting a 2001 Oscar Award for *Crouching Tiger, Hidden Dragon*. Experiencing fear gave Michelle Yeoh the sense that she was challenging herself in a fundamental way. It seems that Yeoh does not want to play it safe in her movies or in life. In the movie *Crouching Tiger, Hidden Dragon,* she performed her own stunts, risking a serious injury that eventually occurred. I believe it was this sense of risk, of facing fear, that made making the movie for Michelle Yeoh worthwhile.

We all, at varying times and in varying degrees, encounter fear. It is a natural reaction, a survival instinct. All animals and humans are wired for it. In Alex Kozma's book, *Esoteric Warriors*, a ba gua chang martial artist says, "When someone is bent on destruction and coming for you then you have a choice to survive or not. We are born with an innate survival system in our bodies, we want to live, we don't want to die. That instinct is very pure and is connected to higher consciousness, Tao, or God." Fear is our alert signal that something might be wrong and that we might need to take action. "We are literally blinded by emotion, concentrating only on surviving the situation by fighting or fleeing," writes Ciaramicoli. Without fear we are inadequately prepared for risks. We need our fear. We need our fear so that we are in touch with dangerous situations and can make adequate judgments as to risk factors. Without fear we would not be prepared for surprises that may harm us. Without fear we would not be circumspect and we would be easy targets for victimization. It is fear that can touch our intuition and trigger our natural responses. It is never good to deny fear or any other emotion because they are our access to intuitively understanding a situation and what we need to do. But fear becomes a problem when it dominates or controls our responses, when we cannot act because we become paralyzed by our fear, or when we avoid potentially positive situations because our fear inhibits us.

Access to Courage

IF WE ARE NOT IN contact with our own source of courage, we need to find a way to experience courage in order to locate it and begin to believe in it. The word "belief" gains significance. If you believe it to be so, it will be so, because we tend to manifest our beliefs. If you fully believe that you do not have five dollars in your pocket, you are not going to look for it, even though it might be there. Throughout this chapter, you'll find tools to support the development of healing and discovering your access to courage.

My grandfather taught the power of belief to me. As a child, I remember him telling me countless stories about his life in Zimbabwe, then Southern Rhodesia. He was either the most incredible man in the world or he was the most incredible story-teller. In one such story, he told of a witch doctor who had been murdered on a path close to the village where my grandfather lived. The path was never used because the witch doctor's spirit haunted it. One night my grandfather, somewhat inebriated, was riding back to his hut on a horse. When he came to the fork in the road, he accidentally tried to make the horse go down the wrong path. The horse refused, snorting and backing away. The horse resisted as my grandfather insistently forced him to go the wrong way. Suddenly the horse reared up in terror as the ghost of the witch doctor appeared before them. The horse galloped back down the path to the village, my grandfather barely hanging on.

My grandfather fully believed in the spirit he witnessed that night. He explained to me how voodoo works on people's belief systems: those who believe will surely be affected. Imagine if we harnessed the power of belief and attached it to courage rather than to fear? Belief is an incredibly powerful force. By consciously imagining ourselves feeling courageous and acting courageously, we can begin to believe we are courageous. If you believe it to be so, it will be so.

Afraid to Be Afraid

WHEN HARRY CAME back to live with me, I was confronted with the omnipresent fear that Harry might attack. He had spent eight weeks on the farm in training with Adam Stone, the canine aggression expert, while I had made the trek there three times a week for my training. There, Harry was taught how to listen, but I was taught how to understand dogs, to communicate with them, to deal with difficulties, and to begin to trust myself. Adam taught me how to distinguish myriad dog behaviors. I observed dog behavior for hours while Adam deciphered and made clear to me their body cues. Adam observed my interactions with Harry, pointing out the subtle dance we had created, and taught me how to become a leader. At that stage in my learning, it took constant courage to interact with Harry, as I did not really believe yet that I could do it. Slowly I learned. Slowly I began to believe. Slowly I found my courage to continue.

It is not as though Harry came back to me a totally changed animal, complete with deferential bowing. I wish he had! That would have fed my desire to allow someone else to handle the difficult problems of my life. The incidental guru will never allow me to get off that easy. No, Harry is Harry. He is a handful. He is a character. He is relentless in his pursuit of his deepest desires. (Thank God he came neutered!) I would have to rise to the challenge of creating a relationship with an intimidating dog.

I knew that being afraid might ultimately trigger his fear response. Animals and man are fashioned with a phenomenon researchers call physiological synchrony. Our minds and bodies are "intimately intertwined and interdependent. Our nervous systems, in other words, talk to each other," says Ciaramicoli. He uses wonderful examples in his book *The Power of Empathy*: "When a mother plays with her infant, their hearts begin to beat in time. When you pet your dog, your heartbeat slows down — and so does your dog's."

Harry is so perceptive that I feared he would smell my fear. I was afraid my fear would manifest his bite. How would I get out of this one? I knew what Harry was capable of. I knew Harry didn't know whether he could trust me, and I didn't know whether I could trust him. At times I saw him watching me with trepidation. We were locked in a cycle that I had to get us out of. I could not expect Harry to react differently until I transformed the way I communicated with him. He was the dog and I was the human. I hoped I had better reasoning skills than he.

Our dogs are our mirror. Our dogs behave according to what we do or don't do. That doesn't mean that we are responsible for all their bad or good behaviors. Dogs, like people, have their own predilections. It is how and what we do with those predilections over time that determines what kind of relationship we will have. For the most part, we have the ability to create different relationships when we fully appreciate and understand what effect we can have on others.

The Journey Begins

I WAS COMING TO the realization that I might effectively transform my relationship with Harry and we might some day come to understand each other. I was terrified but willing to begin the journey. How long it would be I didn't know. At night I still had dreams of Harry appearing docile one minute, curling back his lips to reveal his stunningly sharp teeth to pounce on me the next. I would wake in a cold sweat. Harry would be asleep curled in a ball looking angelic.

I became steeped in the themes of fear and courage. It seemed that everywhere in my life fear and courage presented themselves to me in endless ways to be observed, analyzed, understood, experienced. They presented themselves to me in movies, books, and conversations. They followed me to Northern Ireland on a peace mission. I can still feel the intensity of being lined up through the machine-gun sights of British officers riding past in army Saracens and of being swept up in a spontaneous street riot where clubs, tear gas, and rubber bullets were the tools of suppression. They presented themselves in my dreams, at seminars, and in the issues my clients were currently engaged in. I could not get away from them. They followed me around like a shadow image.

Past Meets Present and the Future Becomes Now

LIKE A ZEN KOAN in which the mind is thrust into a place where the usual logical responses have no relevance, the dog's world, according to Adam's teaching method, must be turned upside down in order to open the dog's mind to a new learning. This rang a bell with my psychological training and the supposition that people often feel extremely confused while perched on the precipice of a new learning. For example, I recall very clearly not too long ago feeling utterly confused and unable to articulate my experience as I was writing this book. I spoke to Alex, my teacher of ba gua chang — the Taoist internal martial art similar to Tai Chi that links a fighting system with the cultivation of spirituality, subtle energies, and consciousness — who laughed and laughed and said, "Great! You know nothing. That is wonderful. Truly wonderful." No matter how often I experience a state of utter confusion, I rarely embrace it. Yet it is a necessary step on the journey to new understanding.

During Harry's training, the goal was to create an off-balance mode for Harry so that authentic learning could take place. The first way of altering Harry's reality was by taking away his freedom and putting him into a crate. That really rocked Harry's world. He was used to two or three off-leash walks a day. I loved our walks. I live near the beach and used the walks to clear my mind while I was writing. When Harry lost his freedom, his world changed and his mind opened. Once Harry's mind was open, we began to work on our relationship. It was the step that would create the most profound change in Harry and in me.

I began to look at what was developing between Harry and me. Whenever I felt the least bit uncomfortable, I banished Harry to the other side of the house. Harry went there, slightly uncomprehendingly, but went nevertheless. I had discovered a way to *cope* with my fear and, at the same time, I was establishing my territory, perhaps even becoming a leader in Harry's eyes. I had an effective tool to deal with my fear: boundary training. I redis-covered the courage I had found when I had to face my shyness. I still was afraid of what Harry might do, but now I had some-thing that I could do whenever I felt uncertain of his moods. I felt more confident that I might be capable of something more than merely coping.

Those moments of confidence didn't last. Whenever I felt I was gaining ground with Harry, he would do something that would unnerve me yet again, catapulting me directly into the past. Sometimes what Harry would do was innocuous but it would terrify me nonetheless. For instance, when I came home from work Harry used to "talk" to me while we put our noses together and I patted his head. His talking sounded like a low growl, almost a purr. The beautiful purr that had been an intimate and special conversation between two species became an omi-nous growl to me. I would react as though he had just attacked me, exiling him to the outer reaches of our home. Harry stopped purring for one full year. Recently I realized how I had effectively shut him down, and I lamented the loss of that special communi-cation. A few days after that realization, Harry purred again. It was as though he were waiting for me to be comfortable again with his talking.

At other times Harry's actions were not so innocuous. Harry was still loath to give up found objects, and he would try his intimidation tactics on me. His intimidation had worked bril-liantly in the past; he was sure it would work again on me.

During his rehabilitation, I would remind myself that that was then and this is now. I was no longer a victim of Harry's intimi-dation. If Harry didn't immediately listen to me, I could turn my back and walk away. What Harry would defend to the death one minute would become a discarded, forgotten object the moment I walked away. Turning my back and walking away from Harry became my most effective weapon in my battle for Harry's rehab. It helped me deal with my fear because I didn't have to directly confront an animal that was entirely capable of becoming a snarling, growling, menacing, and biting wild thing. I could let Harry know I would not stay around for that kind of mistreatment and once home he would lose his freedom until he earned it again.

I was taking the first steps towards facing my fears with Harry, learning how to react with a plan that was slowly becoming second nature. I could not have done it without the help of that gifted expert Adam Stone. He was not always an easy teacher to have. He expected commitment, he expected hard work, he expected a certain amount of willingness to enter into the fear in order to overcome it. Adam helped Harry transform the way he related in the world and in so doing helped me transform the way I related as well. In order to find courage and confidence, I had to learn. I knew from other experiences that the will to make a change is only an idea that initiates the first step to creating authentic change. Creating authentic change always entails new learning. I have been fortunate in my life to have always found incredible teachers whenever I entered a new realm of learning. It is almost as though great teachers magically appear in my life, along with books and new friendships.

The techniques that Monty Roberts, the model for *The Horse Whisperer,* uses in his compassionate method of training horses are similar to those used to understand the language of dog and human: of attraction and aversion, trust and dependence, freedom and restriction. I began the program of rehabilitation for Harry. Harry and I moved into the future leaving our traumatic past behind as a lesson to learn from. I had a training program that would help shape our relationship.

Jeffrey Moussaieff Masson says, "To a certain extent we are the jailers of our dogs, since any freedom they achieve must be acquired by wheedling it out of us. This is one good reason they learn to read us so well. Survival dictates that dogs learn about us and learn to play us to some extent. Dogs must learn to negotiate whatever freedom they achieve within the confines that we assign them. They seem to accept this control we exercise over them as the way things are. Dogs who rebel we call problem dogs. Perhaps they are merely independent thinkers, wondering why they should accept the status quo."

Moussaieff Masson could easily have been writing about Harry in this passage. Harry is a master manipulator and has learned to play me well, to mold me to his particular needs. By the time I would catch on to one of his games he had already moved on to another. I cannot take Harry for granted nor what I have achieved with him. I still have to stay aware of what Harry is doing, because he is so opportunistic. Harry continually challenges the status quo and he needs a very good reason to listen to a human, even the human whom he lives with each day.

Harry seems more sensitive to my undertones than I am to his. He behaves like a cheeky devil when I am stressed. He seems aware that something is bothering me and my attention is elsewhere. Harry takes advantage. He runs rampant and my frustrated attempts to get him to listen remain unheeded. He has a blast at those times, and I am only just learning the subtle nuances in my own behavior that tip him off. Harry is a better barometer of my moods than any internal signal I have discovered. I am humbled at his ability. I always believed myself to be sensitive and intuitive, fairly aware, but discovered instead that compared to Harry, I am obtuse and sometimes fear-ridden.

While Harry has learned to read me well, I have often missed the signs and signals of Harry's moods. I would choose the wrong times to confront Harry and make a point, upsetting our delicate balance of the time. I often misjudged the motives for his behaviors, interpreting a growl as disrespect and feeling outraged by it, or interpreting his resistance to commands as out-and-out insolence and insisting he listen to me. In the past, Harry would revert to growls and bites to make his point. Gradually, I learned that

Harry's growls and resistance were expressions of his confusion about my behavior, as though Harry were trying to correct me and teach me how to be a better leader. I began listening to what Harry was trying to teach me. I finally stopped thinking I had to confront my fear through Harry, and realized I had to begin to confront some of the deepest and most hidden aspects of myself.

Many people today seem to be out of sync with what were once natural emotional responses. In our attempts to gain mastery over ourselves, we have instead suppressed our emotions to the degree that we don't know what we feel anymore or how to respond. With animals as responsive as dogs, it can be detrimental to the relationships that we are trying to build. Adam Stone says about dogs and fear, "Unlike modern humans who need to experience terror before we outwardly act fearful ... dogs use instinct, pure and simply, nonjudgmental and constant." Staying in touch with our feelings, our responses, and our experience — not suppressing them, yet not necessarily acting them out — is how we build authenticity in our relationships and in ourselves.

Dogs seem to pick up on the emotional states of others, whether they be fear, anxiety, or relaxed confidence. This may explain why confident dog owners seem more capable of establishing leadership with less work than anxious owners who are constantly worried about their performance. I unfortunately fell into the latter category. Elizabeth Marshall Thomas in *The Social Lives of Dogs* says to owners of problem dogs, "Relax. Dogs are extremely sensitive to human tension, especially when they themselves are the cause."

Facing Emotional Fears Courageously

MANY OF US LIVE our lives dominated by emotional fears without acknowledging or perhaps even being aware of how pervasive they can be. We stay distant from our loved ones out of fear. We fear animals, snakes, or spiders, even when they don't pose a threat. Out of fear, we don't say the things we need to say. We don't do the things we want to do. We fear failure. We fear success. We fear being disliked or looking stupid. We fear we will not adequately provide for our families or ourselves. As children, we fear the dark, as adults, we fear being alone. We fear ourselves and we fear what we might be capable of. We fear others and what they might do to us. Our fears have lost their original contexts.

Consider how often we hold back our true feelings from others because we fear the consequences of speaking up. We may feel hurt and not want to admit to it, only to discover upon talking about it that the hurt was a misunderstanding and could easily be resolved. A client of mine described a scenario wherein a misunderstanding could have grown to epidemic proportions. She chose to deal with it courageously rather than allow the issue to fester. She had made a telephone call that angered a coworker and subsequently he had distanced himself from her. She was perplexed by his reaction. She arranged to meet him to discuss the issue. It turned out that a week earlier she had inadvertently shut him down in a meeting with the CEO, and another coworker had made a comment that led him to believe she was undermining him to others. She clarified the intention of her telephone call, and they devised a plan whereby neither would feel undermined in meetings. That was enough for both of them to continue their work towards the betterment of the company. I like this example of how courageously communicating problems can clear up misunderstandings and hurt feelings to generate a positive outcome.

We have so many fears that we come to accept as inevitable, rather than questioning if there could be another possibility. We may like someone but be afraid the feeling isn't mutual so hold back, missing an opportunity to create a friendship or romance. We may hold back feelings that we believe unpleasant, fearing the impact that unleashing them may have. Being sensitive to the impact of our words and deeds is essential in respecting others, but we can lose the purpose of this sensitivity and miss out on opportunities for deeper understanding and closer connections with others.

Self-censorship can be invoked for numerous reasons: to protect someone from our less-than-generous feelings or to protect ourselves from an unpleasant reaction, ridicule, appearing silly, or rejection. These protective behaviors may seem to keep us safe from perceived risks, but what they really do is imprison us, keep us from being authentic to ourselves and to others.

It takes courage to reveal deep feelings. It is not always easy to communicate effectively. In *Music of the Mind,* Darryl Reanney writes beautifully about the inadequacy of words: "Speech is a frail reed reaching out across the gap of minds; it makes contact possible but the message it carries is crippled by the very act of crossing."

The Impact of Our Words and Deeds

COURAGEOUS COMMUNICATION is not about opening your mouth and allowing whatever is there to tumble out regardless of its impact. That is irresponsible. If we are to be responsible for our communications, we must consider what purpose our words will serve, what consequences they will hold. Will it be to heal someone or hurt them, to put them down because they have put us down? Will it be to inform? To make someone (or ourselves) look better? Will our words communicate how much we care, or will our words conceal it? Our communication can keep us hidden as much from ourselves as from others if we allow it.

We need to question what affect our actions will have before we act. And we need to dig underneath our self-deceptions to ferret out our motivations. If this feels particularly difficult, then all the more reason to explore what your motivations are. By definition what is unconscious cannot be conscious, so it can be useful to enlist the help of a trusted friend to help you identify the impact your words and deeds have on others. Try to be brutally honest with yourself. Try to put your feelings in the rawest of terms. Try to listen to what a friend says when you have affected them in a way you had not intended. So if you are seething with jealousy towards a friend, admit it. Don't make excuses for yourself.

Like others, I have not always paid attention to the impact of my words and deeds. It is a discipline that requires continual practice. We communicate in many different ways, and we need to pay attention to what messages our actions give. The husband who gives his wife chocolates on Valentine's Day, though she has made it clear she feels overweight, is on a diet, and wants support in losing weight, is certainly sending a message. The message is, "I don't really care about you or what is important to you." The wife who spends the family's money on her own clothes when there are other priorities is sending a message to the other family members that she feels they are less important to her than herself. We have to really look at the messages that we give to those we say are important to us. We need to make sure we let them know they are important to us. Our words and our actions need to be in harmony to convey to others what we want. If your words say, "I love you," and your actions do nothing to support the words, then you must seriously consider what you want your message to be. Becoming aware of the messages you are sending helps you understand what you might need to change.

Many couples who come to me for therapy say they love each other and want to stay together, but everything that they do sends a different message. Their bond is not being strengthened by their actions but being slowly frayed away until only a thin strand is holding things together. With courageous communication, couples can begin to sort out how they really feel about each other and their partnership. It can be extremely difficult but it is the only way to the truth for each person. The courageous muscle is stretched again and again in therapy as we look at ourselves honestly and communicate honestly.

It is impossible to fool a dog like Harry with an ambiguous action. He catches it immediately. If you say to Harry, "Don't do that," but you don't really mean it, he is unlikely to obey you. With Harry, the clarity comes in the directness of the communication, the consistency of the communication, the action that supports what was communicated. Harry is not encumbered with the masks and pretensions that humans use to obscure intent.

Intention

WHEN WE BEGIN to appreciate the interconnectedness of people, animals, and the world we live in, our actions become directed towards what is "right," rather than what will serve the immediate moment. "Rightness is to be measured always by the degree to which it serves the good of the whole, not the ambition of the part," writes Darryl Reanney in *Music of the Mind*. If we try to keep that simple construction in mind when we act, we will most often act in ways that maintains our integrity and the intensity of our focus. The Dalai Lama writes in *Ancient Wisdom, Modern World*, "It also becomes apparent that our every action, our every deed, word and thought, no matter how slight or inconsequential it may seem, has an implication not only for ourselves, but for all others too." This concept is called "dependent origination."

Like a pebble thrown into a pond, the reverberations of our actions keep reaching out until they are no longer discernible, but the effects live on nevertheless. For every action we take, there is a consequent reaction, and for that reason we must always be mindful of what we do. If you yell at your child in the morning before he goes to school, he may still be upset when he arrives at school. In his first classroom, he writes a spelling test and is thinking about how he didn't mean to spill the milk at the breakfast table when he was fiddling with the baseball he forgot he wasn't allowed to have on the table in the first place. He misspells "conceit" as "conciept" and remembers the rule that i comes before e except after c, but he is still upset so he just looks at what letter he wrote after the c and afterwards changes all subsequent spellings of words with "cei." The test is corrected in class immediately and he gets 5 right out of 40. He tells himself that he is dumb and at the end of the day forgets the math book he needs to prepare for the test the next day because he will probably fail that too anyway. The sound of the yelling died out long before the effects. This might seem like an extreme example, and many children are quite able to let the rants of a stressed-out adult roll off their backs without such lasting effects, but through my many years of work with children in my psychotherapy practice, I have found that they are often sensitive to what we adults feel are innocuous statements.

Why did courage become so important for the rehabilitation of Harry and the wholeness of me? Whenever we get stopped in life, we become limited and ultimately unfulfilled. I was limited by the belief that I would be unable to train a dog that bit. Whenever the training got difficult, such as when Harry would stubbornly, obstinately, belligerently resist, I would be tempted to give up. I would fall into the fear that he might bite me, that I couldn't train Harry because there was something inherently wrong or inadequate about me. I would feel incapable of out-thinking my dog, who had nothing better to do with his life than make mine miserable, running off to have a great time, before coming back to me to enjoy all the fruits of a warm, loving home. It was merely one instance among many of how I would not challenge myself when I felt the going got too tough.

The lesson from Harry ended up being less about confronting his ugly wolfish grin and more about confronting my own internal fears that continually stop me from achieving what I set out to achieve. With every challenge I face and push through, whether I am successful or not, I gain greater access to courage and greater confidence for the next challenge.

With the depth of courage I discovered through Harry, I finally located the courage to write, to speak up, to be stupid, and to be intelligent. I was just as fearful about being intelligent. How stupid is that? I feared I might make other people feel uncomfortable if I knew more than they knew or showed them up. I became adept at ignoring inaccuracies, inconsistencies, and outright mistakes in others — paradoxical for someone addicted to perfection. I had to count myself among the many people who create webs of inconsistencies to keep themselves hidden as much from themselves as from others.

In my arsenal of fears was the fear of loss driving me to base decisions on survival instead of on choice, the fear of retaliation pushing me to not stand my ground, the fear of looking bad inhibiting my actions, words, and responses, the fear of failure inhibiting my action, and the fear of success holding me back. Not a bad list for someone who hadn't considered herself a fearful person.

The Courage to Be Wrong

FOR YEARS I WAS SO shy that I never said anything. I remember as a child hiding behind my mother's skirt. I remember everyone constantly trying to coax me out into the open, get me talking when strangers were around. I wouldn't comply. I didn't want to be seen, and I didn't want to say anything. I was overly critical of myself and allowed that fear to keep me from doing what I wanted to do. Fairly recently, around the time insights kept crashing in on me, I was driving my car, listening to the radio. The radio announcer said something that sounded really stupid. I was extremely critical of him because he is usually articulate and intelligent. Then I got it. I am so critical that my expectation of others and of myself for perfection will never be met. Why not accept everyone, including myself, for his or her foibles. In fact, foibles are what great comedy is all about — and I love laughing. I thought, if he can sound stupid, then why can't I? It was a very freeing moment.

Physical Courage

MY GOOD FRIEND, also named Cindy, has always been afraid of activities associated with physical risk, though she really wanted to learn how to dive, scuba dive, and ski. Cindy decided to face her fear, so she took lessons. Taking lessons is an excellent way to overcome fears. Cindy learned how to scuba dive and to ski and she experienced an incredible sense of accomplishment. Cindy had engaged in a learning process that allowed her to gain the physical skills necessary to master scuba diving and skiing while facing her fears one step at a time. Cindy was bridging her knowledge gap to overcome her fears. However, Cindy had still not challenged her fear of diving into a cold northern lake.

Emotional Courage

CINDY DID NOT LACK the knowledge or the skill needed for diving, but something was holding her back. Through the discovery of her own source of courage, Cindy challenged herself to dive that summer. At that time, Cindy was in a relationship with a man who claimed he was commitment phobic. The act of diving into the lake made her feel so strong within herself she said to the man, "It is time for you to decide whether or not you want to walk with me in this world, because I am walking on. You need to stop thinking about what you are afraid of, stop talking about your fear, and just put your shoes on and walk if you don't want to lose me." Cindy took a giant leap into the cold, clear water and it gave her the strength to take a riskier leap into the unknown waters of her relationship. She knew that what she said to the man would either move the relationship to the next stage or end it completely.

In *If Life is a Game, These Are the Rules*, Cherie Carter-Scott cites a story from her own life in which she is afraid to dive into water. She didn't feel afraid of physical injury or failure, she was "simply afraid in the way that humans often are, when they stand poised to jump, metaphorically or literally, into the unknown." Once she realized that there was only one way to do this and that was to just do it, she did: "What fears stand in your way? Bring them to light so that you can loosen their hold over you. Fears, real or imagined, only impede you. Banish them so that you may learn the lesson of courage and create a life that you desire."

One Step at a Time

DURING A RECENT conversation with a friend, I became aware of just how often fear enters my world and the subtle ways I allow it to distort my actions. I realized that I had refrained from saying something important because I feared the potential impact it might have on our relationship. I had actually convinced myself that the issue was unimportant, until that moment of realization that I had altered my actions to avoid the issue.

It is almost humorous how I, like many people, allowed fear to control me, though I would object vociferously if I felt someone else trying to exert control over me. It became clear that behind everything that stopped me was fear.

It also became clear to me in yoga class. When we ask our bodies to stretch beyond what we are normally comfortable with, our bodies immediately become tense and we cannot go much farther. Yet when we relax, it is surprising what we can accomplish. I was shocked one day to find I could do a backbend just by breathing into the resistance and relaxing. The following week I was unable to repeat it. My fear stepped in and stopped me. I could almost hear my brakes squealing, "Stop! What are you doing? You can't do a backbend! Don't do it!"

When we are anesthetized, our bodies can be moved, twisted, and stretched into almost any position. If our muscles are capable of it when anesthetized, what keeps us from doing it when we are conscious? Fear. We fear we cannot do a backbend or the splits, or touch our toes, so our mind stops our body from performing. We have to train our fear out a little at a time, stretching our muscles bit by bit, convincing ourselves that we can do when conscious what we can do when we are unconscious! This is a good model for developing courage. We train ourselves slowly, convincing ourselves that we can do what we already can do but only fear we cannot.

The Outer Limits

THE WAY WE THINK really does inhibit what we are capable of. Years ago I worked part-time at a school, counseling children with learning and behavioral disabilities. One child I will never forget was an eleven-year-old mentally handicapped girl who was so incredibly physically strong she could pick up metal filing cabinets filled with textbooks like they were matchboxes filled with balsa wood. She could punch a hole in a concrete reinforced wall and giggle afterwards. I am quite sure that time has not made me exaggerate this young girl's feats of physical prowess.

We learn to think certain limiting thoughts about ourselves and this girl didn't have any of the ordinary restraints on her thinking. She didn't recognize she was young and small and supposed to have no strength. In fact, she struggled with the simple concepts of self that young children learn fairly naturally through observation and exploration. This is similar to the capabilities we possess under hypnosis, when the everyday restraints or beliefs our conscious minds impose are released.

Obviously we need some limits or restraints on our thinking, otherwise we might all be running around acting like King

Kong, picking up cars and whipping them about our heads. But what I am getting at is how those limiting thoughts imprison our minds and limit the capabilities that are truly within our realm of possibility.

My sister one day discovered her beloved dog, Rasta, a one-hundred-and-thirty-pound Bouvier des Flandres dangling by his choke chain after somehow sliding through a gap in the railing of a second-story deck. She reached down and pulled him up and over the railing, saving his life. Who knows how he managed to slip his bulky body through the deck railing in the first place? But perhaps more remarkable is how my sister managed to lift his struggling bulky weight up over a railing. There are countless stories of emergency situations in which people suddenly locate reserves of power, stamina, strength, and courage. German concentration camps and imprisonment as a prisoner of conscience, fires, and accidents have all given birth to such incredible feats of courage.

Learning how to deal powerfully with fear triggered my emotional fears. Fears of not being capable. Fears of not being capable of building the relationship with Harry I desired, of not being capable of just about anything I really wanted to do that challenged me in fundamental ways. I hate to say it, but I was not up to the challenge of my own life. I was living a life that was less than what I was capable of because I feared I was incapable and I allowed that fear to rule.

Our Deepest Fear

NELSON MANDELA SAID, "Our deepest fear is not that we are inadequate. Our deepest fear is that we are powerful beyond measure. It is our light, not our darkness that frightens us. We ask ourselves, 'who am I to be brilliant.' Actually who are we not to be."

I believe that those who find within themselves an unceasing source of courage often become world leaders. Mahatma Gandhi, the Dalai Lama, Nelson Mandela, and Martin Luther King — these leaders had the courage of their convictions and therefore no longer needed to engage in ruthless behaviors or power struggles, or experience defeat in achieving their dreams. They had the courage to believe that what they were doing was right and the rightness of their choices were illustrated by the fact that their choices benefited the whole rather than merely their part. We also can find our own source of courage by constantly facing our fears.

Often we think of great leaders as profoundly different from ourselves. We believe they are brilliant beyond imagination, fiercely independent and fearless, but I think that detracts from their greatness. Most leaders have great vision, surround themselves with remarkable people, and possess an inner intensity that drives their perseverance to achieve their goals. They drive ceaselessly towards their goals, even when the results of their goals may be uncertain. I believe it is this dedication that makes them seem fearless, for when something stops them, they find the courage to carry on despite adversity. Often we speak of fearlessness when what I think we really mean is the capacity to be with fear while finding our courage to act.

The Hero's Journey

WHENEVER A RADICAL shift in consciousness occurs, what once was dies away and something new emerges. Joseph Campbell, an American author and teacher known for his work on myths and comparative mythology, refers to this as the hero's journey. It is in the hero's journey that one leaves the realm of what is safe and secure and confronts the new frontiers of the self. It is that journey that I was compelled to embark on when confronted by the obstinate belligerence of Harry. I had to stop confronting Harry and begin confronting my own fears and myself. It was then that I became open to learning. It was then that I learned how to communicate with Harry. And in so doing I learned and continue to learn about myself.

Indigenous North American Natives have a ceremony known as a vision quest. The idea as I understand it is to stay alone outside, with the minimum requirements for health, perhaps some Native medicine, with no distractions, no ordinary comforts or safe retreats, to discover one's true self and true strength. In time, the questor will be delivered a vision that will have profound relevance for his or her life. Guess what most people deal with? Fear. The initial fear is usually of being outside at night with wild animals. Gradually, the questor realizes that the animals are not terribly interested in humans and the attention shifts from the fears of the outer world to the fears of the inner world. As the vision quest enters into the deeper, more spiritual aspects, it is the fear of being alone with the self that is ultimately what one has to come to grips with. This psychological process is an important and central part of the larger spiritual quest.

Mark Epstein, a M.D. and psychoanalyst, says, "It is a paradox of self-discovery that we can know ourselves only by surrendering into the void." In Epstein's wonderful book *Going to Pieces Without Falling Apart,* he writes of "a Buddhist perspective on wholeness." What Epstein discusses is facing the fear of emptiness through discovering the capacity to be alone. He believes that in today's Western world, we have an aversion to feeling empty. We make emptiness a sign that something is wrong and we have to immediately fill ourselves. Instead of finding a way to fill ourselves, we need to find a method of being alone with ourselves, of overcoming the fears that being alone brings. In that state we will discover who we are.

A few years ago, when I first left my husband of twelve years, I lived by myself in a small bachelor apartment. I couldn't stand being alone. I wanted to be distracted from myself. But, like the vision questor, over time I came to confront my fear of being alone, began to learn about myself, and found I not only could be alone but I enjoyed it. Instead of wanting to be distracted from myself, I began feeling resentful of the distractions outside myself. It was only then that I began to write from my heart.

"When we are afraid to relax the mind's vigilance, however, we tend to equate this floating with drowning and we start to founder ... In this fear, we destroy our capacity to discover ourselves in a new way. We doom ourselves to a perpetual hardening of character, which we imagine is sanity but which comes to imprison us." Mark Epstein seems to be describing the resistance we experience when being alone with ourselves. The Native ceremony of the vision quest confronts the fears that can imprison us. We don't all have to experience a vision quest, but it illustrates what many of us experience when we do not challenge ourselves. We feel empty and fear it. We then fill up all available space and never get a chance to find out who we are. No wonder so many people in the Western world talk about feeling lost, empty, and meaningless. We have become addicted to distractions, our televisions often occupy the central position in our homes, our radios drone in the background, and we eat when we aren't hungry and not necessarily for nutrition. We cannot even get into an elevator without having a musical environment created for us.

To Go Willingly into the Unknown

BRITISH PSYCHOANALYST D.W. Winnicott teaches that to go willingly into the unknown was the key to living a full life. If a parent provides a child with "good enough ego coverage," meaning the parent has given the child the capacity to feel safe while being alone, the child can enter the unknown feeling secure, without fear. Winnicott believes that a mother needs to not only take care of her infant's physical and emotional needs but just as importantly be able to leave the infant alone to experience life in his or her own way. If a parent interferes too much with a child's personal experience, the child may not adequately develop a capacity to be alone.

When a parent is either overbearing or unavailable, children must use their mental energy coping. As a consequence, children don't get the opportunity to explore themselves. They are left feeling false or empty. Winnicott believes that to go into the unknown when the bond to the parent has been compromised reminds us of how unsafe we once must have felt. Winnicott believes that to get over this fear of emptiness, "a new experience in a specialized setting" is necessary. Winnicott often refers to the fear of emptiness as the sense of the infant being in an infinite fall.

Human infants are dependent on their parents for their very survival and are hardwired to notice when they are not safe. The experience of fear triggers a response of crying out to alert the parents that they need protection. I believe Winnicott is talking about a sense of security that allows many of us to go with courage in the face of our fears. In the absence of security, the ability to find a source of courage is underdeveloped. The greater the degree of security, the easier it is for us to gain access to our courage. We can humbly bow to those in our midst (and I am thinking of some of my clients now) who have had to summon from the depths of nowhere the courage to gain some small sliver of security for themselves to grow one small step at a time.

I believe the fear experienced by many adults suffering from panic and anxiety disorders is either caused by or exacerbated by the lack of an early sense of security that Winnicott describes. I was recently working with a lovely young woman who suffered from panic attacks, which began the week after her mother died. The panic attacks had severely affected and restricted her life during the past seven years. She could not go shopping in an indoor mall. She could not drive long distances. She could not eat in restaurants. Her panic attacks threatened her ability to maintain her job. This woman is beginning to live life again without the affliction of panic attacks by exploring her own experiences in a therapy setting that provides safety. After her mother's death, the young woman had become responsible for her younger sibling. A few years later, she became a teacher of young children. This woman experienced the loss of her mother and the absence of her father with the premature responsibility of a sibling as overwhelming. She felt unable to ask for help from her friends, nor does she feel confident that she can manage "all alone." She is discovering her capacity to be alone by learning to accept the support of her friends. She no longer experiences the overt symptoms of the panic attacks and is working towards a full recovery.

Courage and Power

GARY ZUKAV SAYS in his book *The Seat of the Soul,* "You lose power when you are threatened by another person, or other people. You lose power when you distance yourself from your fellow humans out of resentment or bitterness, or a sense of disappointment or unworthiness or superiority. You lose power when you long for something or someone, when you grieve and when you envy another. Beneath all of these is fear ...."

Zukav believes that the "human emotional system can be broken down into roughly two elements: fear and love. Love is of the soul. Fear is of the personality ... and behind fear is powerlessness." When confronted with fear we most often freeze or flee. Where is the power in that?

Fear is insidious. It manifests itself in ways that keeps us from living lively, passionate, energetic lives. There is nothing powerful about fear when we allow it to rule our existence. Find your source of courage and you find your power. Find your power and you no longer need to control or dominate or engage in power struggles.

Power Struggles

WE ENGAGE IN POWER struggles when we fear we might lose something. By attempting to deal with Harry's aggressive possessive problem head on, we became embroiled in a power struggle for domination that Harry is always bound and determined to win. Jeffrey Moussaieff Masson talks about how we as humans interpret issues of dominance based on our human constructions of dominance and hierarchy that we create in our corporate boardrooms, universities, and governments. He explains that what we as dog owners may describe as dominance may bear little resemblance to how a dog pack or wolf pack creates and maintains its social order. When owners talk about their dogs as dominant, they often seem proud of the quality and equate it with leadership.

Dominance in dogs is the propensity to want to overpower other dogs, to mount, to posture, to fight when challenged — or even instigate fights — and perhaps to be stubborn when responding to commands. These do not seem to be the factors that contribute to dominance in a dog pack and certainly not to leadership. Not all dominant dogs become leaders and not all leaders are dominant dogs.

If size and strength were a decisive factor for dominance, then the bigger the dog, the more likely it is to be dominant, but that does not seem to be the case. I know a Great Dane named Virgil who never displays what we normally consider dominant behavior in his group of dog friends. Virgil goes along with what the other dogs want to do. He doesn't mount them. He doesn't posture. Moussaieff Masson suggests that wisdom plays a part in dominance, that intelligence and cunning and perhaps even the ability to avoid fights contribute to dominance. I believe the qualities that he talks about are the qualities that give rise to leadership in a dog or wolf pack. An air of confidence may communicate more to subordinate dogs than we are aware of. My friend

Jennifer's dog, Buddy, can stop young, aggressive dogs in mid-flight by merely being.

I have had so many discussions with dog owners who talk about the importance of wresting control and dominance over the dog. After my experimentation and experience, I tend to prefer the more relaxed style of leadership that comes with the confidence of establishing a trusting bond and respect, rather than leadership through subjugation. Elizabeth Marshall Thomas, writer of dog books, discusses how our treatment of animals, and of dogs in particular, is indicative of how we think of them. She says, "I believe the needless insistence on dominating dogs springs from our society's dog fascism, and the very nature of our relationship with dogs inspires this. Dogs are slaves, whether we like it or not. We buy them and sell them, we legally kill them for reasons that no dog would understand, and we control their reproduction by removing their wombs or testicles."

Human beings tend to subjugate what they fear, and they fear what they don't understand. Understanding an animal takes some understanding of the self and an ability to reach out beyond the self to communicate in a language other than words — the language of action and intention. With our animal as well as our human relationships, staying out of power struggles is an integral part of building trusting and respectful bonds.

The Power to Invoke Fear

DEPENDING ON YOUR perspective, Harry and I were either a bad match or a perfect match. His fears and my fears were totally complementary to each other. Harry's method of intimidation, growling and snarling threats to get his world to go the way that he wanted, seems archetypal of how bullies hide their fears by intimidating others. Harry was quite willing to do whatever it took to get people to comply with his wants, and he had obviously learned that intimidating people worked. Like a spoiled child, Harry had become a master of manipulation and I his unwitting dupe.

Though Harry appeared fearless, I believe he feared that humans weren't trustworthy or able to be leaders, and he knew they certainly didn't clearly communicate what they expected him to do. Harry's attitude suggested that he felt he was better off on his own than trusting humans to make any sense at all, though if they gave him food and shelter he would tolerate them as long as they didn't frustrate his desires.

This could be why Harry ended up an abandoned dog. He had an attitude problem: he didn't listen to or respect humans, he was not naturally deferential, and when he felt his human needed some correction, he would feel compelled to correct in the only manner he knew — biting. Perhaps there is leadership in Harry after all! Harry actively engaged in teaching me what he needed me to learn. Harry would growl a warning when I didn't understand him and bite when I pushed him. He was pretty clear, now that I think about it in his terms. There are some dogs who are soft spirits and others who possess strong spirits. Harry has a strong spirit and will not back down from a fight. A confrontation for Harry is an opportunity for a fight. He never entertains submission.

Harry has a friend, Tova, a big-bodied babe. Tova is a shepweiler, a mix of rottweiler and shepherd. She outweighs Harry by perhaps twenty to thirty pounds, but she possesses a soft spirit and sweet soul. One day when she was visiting Harry, I asked them to leave the room. Tova high-tailed it out in an instant with her head and tail low. She looked at me submissively as though I frightened her with the power and authority of my voice. Harry didn't move, giving me a standard Dirty Harry look that said, "Go ahead. Make my day." That was when I realized that my problems with Harry weren't *all* my problems.

Harry was a problem dog with a powerful spirit that just wouldn't submit to a demand. A softer-spirited dog will, if not immediately at least eventually, submit, but a strong-spirited dog will resist with everything he is made of. With Harry, everything became a power struggle. Harry is a hardy animal well equipped for life on the streets. As with abused children, some dogs will submit in an attempt to appease the angry aggressor, others will refuse, preferring to accept whatever blow is dealt, creating a crusty exterior, learning how to fight, and waiting for the moment they may exact revenge or attain their freedom.

Harry refuses to submit. I will never forget when I was first taught how to make Harry lie down. I had bruises and little bites all over my legs and arms. Harry would not lie down. My trainer showed me how to pull rank and make him do it. I pulled on the leash. I stood on the leash. I kneeled on the leash and went for rides around my apartment while I struggled to get Harry down. I hate sometimes being confronted with how I misunderstood Harry so profoundly. Harry will fully cooperate with a human when he feels trust, feels valued and respected. Harry was not ready for the vulnerability inherent for animals in lying down. Harry didn't know me yet and did not trust me enough to lie down. Forcing him to do it just made Harry more insistent on fighting me in later battles.

My vet, Dr. Young, discovered Harry's nature after attempting (with five sturdy assistants) to pin him down and get a muzzle on him in order to take a blood test, all to no avail. When Dr. Young gave up on the muzzle and had one assistant just *be* with Harry without restraining him, Harry cooperated. He was still frightened but felt better about allowing Dr. Young to look in his ears and poke him with a needle to extract blood. Dr. Young came out of the examining room with a smile and told me that Harry just needs to be respected, needs to retain his pride, and that is when you get cooperation. Harry appeared relieved trotting out behind him. Dr. Young explained that some dogs have to be firmly held to get cooperation and others cannot allow themselves to be restrained. Harry belongs to the latter group. Dr. Young impressed me with his understanding.

Harry may have learned at an early age how to intimidate humans. He was either an adorable puppy who got away with murder and who grew up to be quite large and rule the roost through looking cute, being intimidating, growling, biting, and flatly refusing to listen to any direction, or he had always been a street dog. If he lived with a family, he may have been turned loose or may have run away. If he had a previous owner, the owner, probably feeling overwhelmed by the dog's belligerent, intimidating, and aggressive behavior, didn't claim Harry in the hope that someone else might find the wily beast, give him a good home, and teach him how to become a responsible member of society.

Harry *seemed* fearless. Off leash he would wander away. He would approach any dog, any number of dogs, in any situation. He would leap off a high precipice without hesitation. He would race tirelessly and dive heedlessly into the lake. It was only around treasured items and food that Harry's pupils would dilate, his eyes narrow, his mannerisms alter, and his attitude change dramatically. He would stalk an item. He would pace anxiously around his food bowl, his eyes darting nervously, searching for some unknown interloper. He became a different animal. He walked high on his toes as though every sinew of his being was on alert. (I think Harry's toe-walking was the inspiration for Nike's "air" shoes.) The pads of Harry's paws seemed to pump up with air, making him taller, more resilient, and ready to pounce. He recognized no one at those times, and became unrecognizable.

I can say that, unfortunately and unwittingly, I reinforced Harry's aggressive behavior with a tennis ball by not addressing the problem. I felt helpless to do anything so I listened to anyone and everyone about how to deal with what I believed to be Harry's dominant behavior. Some people told me I had to begin to confront the problem and never back down to Harry. Some suggested I physically challenge Harry by taking him down and lying on top of him — the alpha roll. One dog owner warned me that the alpha roll might lead to a dog bite, since the dog would surely see it as a direct challenge he could not back down on. (That advice I should have listened to, and it made perfect sense to me, but I had become convinced that I needed to overpower Harry, to be something different than what I was in order to gain control of my out-of-control dog.)

Harry was afraid. He didn't trust me yet. He didn't even really know me, and I didn't know how to reach Harry. Animosity was building between us and it would eventually erupt into the confrontation that led to Harry biting me.

What could I have done? There are a number of things that I will deal with in this book about Harry's rehabilitation. For now I am going to talk about power struggles, how to recognize them, and how to stay out of them. The more you learn about the process of power struggles and what drives them, the more likely you will be able to swing clear of them in your relationships with friends, spouses, children, coworkers, and strong-spirited dominant dogs. Power struggles happen when there is a profound miscommunication mixed with a fear that something deemed valuable will be lost, be it control, authority, dominance. That is how you recognize the beginning of a power struggle.

For a while it happened constantly with Harry, until I truly understood what a power struggle was and how to disassemble one. The situation that arose when I wanted Harry to go into his crate because he had growled or committed some other equally evil deed is a simple example. Harry dug in his paws and refused to move. I thought, "Ohmigod, I am losing this battle. Harry will usurp me. He will not see me as being in control." How could he? I wasn't in control! I tried to push him into the crate, but Harry was being an obstinate donkey. We were now in the epicenter of a power struggle. I needed to get creative. I knew from experience that Harry would bite when confronted directly, and a power struggle leads to direct confrontation. It was exactly like cornering a wild animal: it leaves little choice but attack or submit. Win or lose.

I took Harry's leash and I put him out the back door, shutting it on a tight leash so that he had to stand. I left him there for about three minutes. (Yeah, I know I am pretty soft.) I opened the door, brought him back in, and led him to his crate. He balked. I took him back outside and left him there for ten minutes. He came back inside and walked freely into his crate and has since.

A similar process exists in human relationships when they become reduced to power struggles. One person (or group) fears he or she might lose something valuable and becomes immutable while the other person (or group) becomes entrenched in a particular position. Couples often become polarized over some issue or another, but once they realize the polarization, they can often resolve their seemingly intractable difference relatively easily. It isn't a matter of giving into the power struggle; that creates a win-lose situation with a power imbalance and one unhappy party. It is not about peace at any price, for that also leads to a disempowerment of one party. It is about discovering an alternative method of disrupting the power. I like the analogy of akido, a marshal art form in which you take the force coming towards you and instead of resisting it, you go with the force and change the direction of that force.

Recognize the process of the power struggle and break the inevitable spiral downwards by getting creative. What can seem to matter so much one day or moment (Harry's life and death battle over a tennis ball) can be irrelevant or at least less important in the next (Harry saw the possibility of losing me when I walked across the field). If it is truly a life and death issue — and some certainly are — the creativity required to disrupt the power struggle is greater. Negotiations of peace processes between countries or territories, mediations of intractable couples in divorces and child-custody battles are just two examples that often require incredible creativity to resolve seemingly irresolvable issues.

Children are masters at pulling their parents into power struggles. Husbands and wives will often find themselves dueling for who will retain the power in the relationship. In such situations, we need to try out various options as a resolution. I had a client whose colleague pulled power struggles with her constantly. She would get locked in. I suggested that she step back from the power struggle and decide what the important issue really was (not who was right and wrong, not what was the right or wrong solution, but what was best for the company) and deal with that. When she presented her potential solution to the impasse, it was factually based on what was best for the growth of the company. Everyone on the executive team embraced the solution and they moved forward after being stopped for several weeks.

I have another client, recently separated from his wife, who would become engaged in power struggles with one of his children. Though he was a CEO of a midsized corporation, he would become completely disempowered by his five-year-old child. His child would have a temper tantrum when it came time to leave the house to go to daycare, to walk the dog, to go shopping, and so on. He had spent a great deal of time trying to reassure her, trying to reason with her, trying to do all the things that a wonderfully sensitive parent would do. I suggested he give her two choices: "Either come with me to the car, or I will have to pick you up and carry you to the car." Of course, she chose the option she thought would stimulate the usual pleading, placating, understanding, and relentless dialogue. She was surprised to discover her father actually whisk her up in his arms and carry her to the car. She was so surprised that she forgot to have her temper tantrum.

My client thought he was out of the woods ... until the next day. Children, like dogs, can be relentless in their pursuits for control, particularly when they have won control in the past. His daughter let him have it with her temper. But he remained resolute to what he needed, to get her to daycare so he could get to work. By the time she got to daycare, she was singing songs. She had temper tantrums about going to bed, eating dinner, and anything else she could think of for about two weeks, then they stopped completely.

Gaining Skills for Courage

I HAD TO LOOK FEAR in the face and get over it or get bitten again. The key to learning how to overcome a realistic, right-in-your-face fear is to gain the skills we need to challenge the fear. It is frightening doing anything that we haven't done before or when we don't know what the outcome might be. So the first step is making sure that we know the areas that we don't know about and recognize the areas we do know about. We need to get trained. We need to learn, practice, do whatever it takes to bridge the knowledge gap that we have identified as keeping us from our original goal, but we mustn't allow the knowledge gap to become just one more thing to be fearful of. Be realistic about the gaps. Many of us are so critical of ourselves, we don't acknowledge the abilities we have. My rule of thumb is if you think you need to learn something in order to proceed, you usually don't, you are just overly critical of yourself, and if you think you don't need to learn something in order to proceed, you probably do.

Often we already know what we need to know to proceed. We stop ourselves with countless justifications as to why we cannot continue. I need another degree in order to write a book. I need to become a dog trainer in order to teach my dog. I need to become a gourmet chef in order to cook my partner a fabulous meal. Then there is the whole area of the things that you don't know about that you don't know you don't know. Sounds confusing but it makes a lot of sense. There was so much I didn't know about training a dog that I didn't know I didn't know. I feel blessed that I found a program that really worked for Harry and a dog expert in Adam Stone who taught me and continues to teach me so much.

How many people do you know who say they want to write?

Writing is easy. You put words to paper. But needing to have those words resonate with others is another issue entirely. That can strike fear into the heart of anyone. What is the nature of that fear? Is it fear of failure? Fear of success? Fear of looking stupid or foolish? It could be any or all of those. When you write, you put pieces of yourself, pieces of your soul, out into the world to be read, digested, analyzed, criticized, challenged, and judged. It takes a while to approach it as a process. When you write or paint or create almost anything, it is a process whereby you are putting something out that you hope will connect with others. It takes courage to take the first step and create something, then it takes courage to recognize that first creations are just the inspiration for the real work, the crafting that follows. Inspirations are a little like love at first sight. It keeps things going for a while but eventually you have to begin developing the relationship, shaping it, understanding it, and challenging what it can become.

I know a man who is a fabulous artist. He became a sign painter because he feared he wasn't good enough to be an artist. His artistry was not concealed even in his sign painting. Each letter he creates has an energy about it that demands attention. However, he feared doing the one thing that would give him fulfillment — his art. He became small in his life. Shy and quiet. He stopped painting even for pleasure. Until recently. He decided to face his fear and show people his work. The response was enthusiastic. To his surprise, it didn't help him to overcome his fear of failure. He still felt fear, though he had expected not to. He remained uncertain about taking the next step in his life.

The enthusiastic response of others doesn't necessarily heal an internal sense of inadequacy. It wasn't until this artist summoned the courage to draw again that his life opened up to new possibilities. The fear didn't go away, but he had found his source of courage that kept him going.

What heals a sense of inadequacy? Being courageous heals it. What do I mean by this? I mean having the courage to do the things you feel inadequate doing. Having the courage to open yourself up to constructive criticism to learn what you need to learn to progress. Having the courage to face up to the areas in which you need practice in order to hone your craft. And having the courage to accept your talents and greatness. Many of us are fearful of accepting praise, as though it is not humble to do so. Some of us fear praise because we feel unworthy. Some of us fear praise because it feels empty to us.

I live with the possibility of fear, but I also now live with confidence. If I had continued to live with fear, I would have to seriously consider giving up Harry. Yet giving up Harry now would be so irresponsible of me. It would be like deciding not to finish the last few steps of climbing Mount Everest just because I felt a little tired. It would be playing it safe. After going through so much together and developing such a bond, I have to keep up what I started. Harry would be devastated to lose another owner. An owner who he has shaped and who has shaped him. Yes, fear rises up in me sometimes like bubbles rising from a drowning man, but those days are becoming few and far between. Now I have the tools I need to deal with fear.

Fear keeps us separate. While I feared Harry, there was no consistent closeness, no authentic connection between us. I was too busy fearing Harry to be able to communicate with him or to love him. When my husband and I experienced difficulties, it was fear that kept us apart. If we could have gotten underneath the fear, understood and respected each other's fear, we may have experienced a different process of separation and divorce. If fear keeps us separate, it is courage that keeps us together. The courage to face our differences, to challenge complacency, and to generate intimacy.

On the flipside, fear can also keep couples together and it can take courage to separate. There are marriages that are built upon fear for a variety of reasons. One reason may be that a partner fears being alone and therefore stays in the marriage even though that marriage may be unsatisfactory or abusive. One partner may fear leaving because the other threatens to harm her (or him) if she (or he) does. Some people marry because they fear so much else in life that marriage becomes a safe haven. In these cases it takes great courage to leave.

Fear contributes to, if not all at least in part, the conflicts in this world. From the conflicts between children (for example, fear of losing a toy) to the conflicts between nations (fear of losing power, resources, or territory). Humans are so arrogant about our self-chosen superior status in the animal kingdom. We are by far the most effective, efficient killers on this planet, except perhaps viruses. I can think of no other species that spends as much time strategizing how to kill its own kind. Although it is true that wild animals often go to great lengths to protect their own territory from transgressors, particularly when times are tough and food is scarce, seldom does it end in the mass destruction or subjugation of an entire group.

We dedicate much of our thinking and resources to protecting our territory and to the mass destruction of others, or at least so that we can threaten it. If we dedicated that much of our time to becoming aware, creating cooperation, promoting the tolerance of differences, engaging those who are disenfranchised, and bringing peace and love into all our lives we would have one awesome world.

Ordinary People in Extraordinary Circumstances

IN A WORLD SHORT of heroes, Rosemary Nelson stands out as a woman synonymous with courage. Rosemary Nelson became an internationally known and respected human rights lawyer against all odds in a country that had oppressed both women and Catholics. The conflict in the North of Ireland of the past thirty years has torn away at the very fabric of daily life.

I met Rosemary Nelson 1998 in a dingy community center in a small Catholic enclave in Portadown, where we sat drinking thick instant coffee, sharing the stories of our lives, and chain-smoking cigarettes. (Though I don't smoke, there it is almost necessary to smoke in self-defense.) The residents of the Garvaghy Road had been on edge for weeks anticipating the yearly triumphalist march of the Orange Order. Two months earlier, twenty-one-year-old Robert Hamill had been kicked to death by an angry mob in the city center while four uniformed officers sat in a Land Rover less than twenty feet away. As the family solicitor, Rosemary announced publicly that she intended to take legal action against the Royal Ulster Constabulary (RUC) officers who refused to intervene and prevent the attack.

I had arrived the day before the annual march, a member of a Canadian delegation of independent international observers of human rights abuses, and was immediately billeted in a local home. I then joined the twenty-four-hour community watch for violence. The residents, hungry for a sympathetic ear, filled each moment with stories of being terrorized, beaten, harassed, and threatened. The previous year the RUC forced a march down the Garvaghy Road.

That was the year that Rosemary had desperately tried to negotiate with uncooperative officers of the RUC before the riot police began to push and shove people sitting silently protesting in the street. Rosemary pushed to the front of the line to hold the slow advance of armored Land Rovers and huge, balaclavaed, body-shielded cops at bay. Rosemary heard the officers taunt the residents. It was a clear provocation. She identified herself as the solicitor for the Garvaghy Road Residents Coalition and asked for the commanding officer, while the residents sat locked-armed in rows on the Garvaghy Road, refusing to allow the Orange Order to march through the heart of their community.

Rosemary Nelson, a small woman in a neatly pressed suit, demanded to speak to someone in the cold wet drizzle of that gray morning. The RUC cursed her in reply and pressed forward. She begged them not to beat the people, she shouted for them to stop advancing before the crowd had a chance to move out of the way. She could see some of her people, neighbors she knew, friends she'd had dinner with, parents whose children played with hers, being crushed by the advancing vehicles. Everything went black for Rosemary after being banged on the side of the head with a police riot shield. She was battered, spit on, punched, and verbally abused. Moments later she ran through the crowds, advising people to take witness to the events. The police then raged through the streets of the community with riot shields, batons, and armored vehicles, seriously injuring hundreds of mothers, fathers, and children.

Rosemary was an extraordinary woman, bright and beautiful, with almond-shaped green eyes, fine-featured and fine-boned. When she moved in her chair, she revealed the disfigured half of her face. Her enemies called her "half-faced Nelson." It was a cruel reminder to Rosemary that one side of her face had been disfigured first by a birthmark and then by a surgeons attempt to correct it. Always with a cigarette in hand, Rosemary spoke with a throaty whiskey growl and a valiant attempt at flippancy. She had a great sense of humor, a little dark, the kind necessary for life in a country engaged in a thirty-year dirty war.

When Rosemary finished law school and she was looking for an articling position, most firms told her that she would never be hired because of her disfigured face. Rosemary persevered. Perseverance was what she had. Perseverance was what made her courageous. Perseverance was what made her brilliant. She found a law firm that took her in and, years later, Rosemary started her own general law practice in Lurgan, close to where she lived with her husband and three children.

She remained in relative obscurity, dealing mostly in family law with both Catholics and Protestants until she took on the case of Colin Duffy, accused of membership in the Irish

Republican Army (IRA). That was when Rosemary first attracted the attention of the RUC. Next came the Hamill family, which hoped for justice for their son Robert. Perhaps the most dangerous case she took on was to become the solicitor for the Garvaghy Road Residents Coalition.

At her chair in the community center, Rosemary gave her time to an endless stream of people who needed her help or support. When Rosemary listened, people felt heard. She had a hard edge detectable in her verbal quips, but she had enormous compassion for people. She touched the lives of so many and gave hope to many more. I can still hear her deep, throaty voice with the slight shake in it that I took as the only evidence Rosemary may have had fear.

At two in the morning in the cold drizzling rain, Rosemary found my close friend, Cindy Wasser, a Toronto criminal defense attorney, and me at an observation post. We talked about what had been happening in the community, the peace agreement, the commission on police, and some of her cases. She told us we should go down to South Armagh to visit one of her friends. We lit more cigarettes. Rosemary took a long pull on hers, appraised us, then pulled a piece of paper from her purse and said, "Look." On the paper was written, "You will die."

Mr. Param Cumaraswamy, UN Special Rapporteur, after an extensive investigation, wrote a condemning report on the harassment and intimidation of defense lawyers by officers of the RUC. In a TV documentary, Mr. Cumaraswamy expressed particular concern for Rosemary's safety. Despite the death threats and intimidation, Rosemary Nelson courageously pressed on with her work. Rosemary believed she could not allow her fear for her own safety to jeopardize people's rights to justice. She would continue her commitment like a dog with a bone to stand up for people who often felt unable to stand up for themselves.

Courage was brought home to me again when, on March 15, 1999, Rosemary Nelson got into her car to drive to work. Twenty minutes later, as her car approached an incline less than a mile from her young daughter's school, Rosemary's car exploded. It was a sophisticated mercury tilt bomb. I will never forget that day. It took only a few hours for the news to wash across the ocean and reach those of us who were blessed to know her. My friend Megan called me to commiserate in grief but ended up having to tell me the tragic news. Rosemary is truly missed. She was and continues to be an inspiration.

On the morning of September 11, 2001, I was walking Harry on the beach when someone walked by and told me the Pentagon and the World Trade Center had been hit by planes. My first reaction was to think that it was untrue, a modern version of H.G. Wells's *War of the Worlds*. My second thought was, "Ohmigod, World War III." I rushed home to watch the events unfold on CNN, and it soon became clear that something horrible had altered the face of North America that morning, the effects reverberating around the world. What also became clear were the numerous stories of ordinary people being courageous in extraordinary circumstances. Although fire fighters and police officers regularly put their lives in danger, we can only imagine what it must have been like for those that gave their lives in valiant attempts to save the lives of others. There are hundreds of stories of ordinary people putting their own lives at risk to help those who were less able during the evacuation of the World Trade buildings.

A few days after September 11, my sister was walking from the subway station near her home in Toronto when she saw a man hitting a young woman and attempting to push her into the street into the path of oncoming traffic. The man was calling the young dark-skinned woman a murderer. No one was doing anything to help, so Wendy rushed over and put herself in between the man and the young woman. She told the man to go away and leave the young woman alone. Wendy said to the man, "You make me ashamed." The man said to her, "I am more white than you," and continued advancing as my sister remained between him and the young woman, whom she directed closer and closer to the door of the subway station. Wendy said, "I am not impressed. Go away." "Make me," he threatened. "You are not worth the effort," she said with disgust. They reached the subway station and the man disappeared. Wendy reassured the young woman who was crying and thanking her for intervening on her behalf. The young woman went into the subway and my sister carried on her way down the street. A few blocks later, Wendy felt that she was being followed and, sure enough, the man was not far behind. Wendy knew she had to think of something or engage in a direct confrontation. She ducked into a crowd entering a store and through to the other side of the building. The man went inside the store, while Wendy changed direction and continued on a different route home.

Wendy definitely has courage and an unwavering sense of justice. Though I don't advise anyone to begin the practice of challenging strangers on the street, since there are many people out there feeling alienated and frustrated to the point of striking out at the next person who gets in their way. Sadly, it is our complacency, our fear of getting involved, our ultimate silence that allows social injustices, both large and small, to continue unchecked.

Biting the Hand That Feeds

CAN I GET CLOSE TO the dog that bit me? Can I trust that? When there are structures put in place beforehand, where trust has an opportunity to build, then my answer is yes. Face the fear. Act with courage. Transformation will emerge as a direct result. The outcome will be a deeper and more profound experience of humanity than will ever come out of an environment of fear, an environment of inequality, of domination and subjugation. "How much more interesting to interact with peers, friends and equals,' writes Jeffrey Moussaieff Masson in *Dogs Never Lie About Love.* We need to stop seeing others and dogs as beings we are superior to and see them instead as beings we are intrinsically connected to. There is no love more incredible than the love that exists between equals.

A Bowl of Courage — A Recipe

IN THE *Wizard of Oz*, the cowardly lion, who has been afraid of his own shadow his entire life, takes a stand in front of the fearsome wizard to beg for some courage to help his new friend Dorothy fight the evil witch and get back to Kansas. The wise wizard recognizes that the lion's request was his first step towards facing his fear and finding his courage. The wizard prepares a bowl of courage for the lion. The cowardly lion thinks he has received some mystical gift from the wizard, something from outside himself to give him courage, but the courage was inside the lion all along and the bowl of courage was really just a bowl of porridge. It was the same for all of the requests made of the wizard. The tinman always had a heart, as evidenced by his sensitivity to others that led him to constantly cry and rust his metal joints. The scarecrow came up with ideas without the brain that he thought he needed to prove his worth. As with the rest of us, all they needed was already inside of them.

Transformation can happen in the context of exploratory conversations that move us, that inspire us, that profoundly affect the way we think or feel about something. In therapy, my clients often begin by saying, "Okay, what do I do? I know what is wrong with me but I just don't know how to change it, get over it, get past it ...." My answer is usually the same. We begin a conversation, a journey, and we will see where that leads.

Finding the source of your courage is a process, somewhat but not entirely magical. Some people seem to have easier access than others do. Here is a plan for developing some courage.

LESSONS IN COURAGE

🐾 Become aware of your fears.

🐾 Develop awareness of the physical manifestations of those fears, such as anxiety, nervousness, butterflies, fainting spells. Take the time to pay attention to your fears and your motives. Spend time alone to hear your inner voices.

🐾 Make a list of your fears and begin with some small ones. Think of courage as a muscle that needs to be stretched little by little.

🐾 Talk about your fears to a trusted friend. Solicit his or her support in facing a fear. Have your friend "hold your hand" in the beginning if that will help.

🐾 Breathe as you feel your physical symptoms manifesting themselves.

🐾 Look for ways other than power struggles to solve issues.

🐾 JUMP! Like jumping into a cold northern lake.

🐾 You can't jump? No problem. Watch how a friend you admire deals with fear and summons courage. There are no failures, only lessons from which to learn.

🐾 Seek out new skills, and practice using them when you are in fear-producing situations.

🐾 Try again to jump.

🐾 Learn to recognize fears that got past you. What held you back? What do you need to face the fear? Support, handholding, help, knowledge, information? Do the things that you feel inadequate doing.

🐾 Jump again and again. Practice. Accept praise for your accomplishments.

Harry on Trust:
A Two-Way Street

A man who doesn't trust himself can never really trust anyone else.

— CARDINAL DE RETZ

WHATEVER I THOUGHT I knew about trust collapsed the day Harry turned on me. Initially, I chose to understand what happened only in terms of what Harry did to me and not how I may have confused Harry with my sudden change of style to direct confrontation. We had betrayed each other. We had broken our tenuous bonds of trust and neither one of us knew what lay ahead.

Trust is elemental to any relationship. When a trust is broken, the relationship is broken and needs to be repaired, if it can be. A broken trust can become a primary issue that reasserts itself in relationships in a never-ending Passion play. When I first adopted Harry from the pound, I held a vision of how our relationship would be. Harry would be the dutiful dog. He would respect me, listen to me, and be my loyal companion. Similarly, we envision how our marriage partner will be or how our child will be. Our partner will be loving, strong, open, and honest; our child will be loving, intelligent, soulful, and sensitive. When our vision of how things "should" be doesn't align with reality, we don't always know how to handle it.

I believed Harry would not betray me. He would not mistreat me. I had no idea then what Harry and I would have to go through to build the kind of bond that I wanted. I never expected the length of time that it would take, or the amount of work it would take, though at the time, I thought I knew.

I believed myself a patient sort of person. I believed I was prepared to dedicate the time required to build a deep and lasting relationship. I believed I was a trusting sort of person and that I was trustworthy. Well! Harry made me throw all my beliefs right into the wind.

I may have trusted others, but on what basis? I never thought to look for evidence of trustworthiness in my dog or in my relationships. I just assumed it. If I were trustworthy, why didn't I ever trust my own instincts and reactions? Any evidence I had about myself I either denigrated or ignored. If I were patient, why did I expect Harry to become my loyal companion in a mere few months? And why did I get so frustrated when he didn't learn quickly enough for me to feel that I was a good enough owner? The guru was doing it to me again. I never expected to learn so much about myself from a dog.

Trust is something that ought to be earned, not blindly taken for granted just because someone holds a place of power or prestige. Trust can easily be abused, consciously or not. Many people maintain an unacknowledged agenda that they impose on others. Doctors and therapists are often granted automatic trust, although that trust can be abused. Similarly, lawyers have access to trust accounts, yet there are those who have absconded with their clients' money. Stay in tune with your intuition because usually your intuition will deliver critical information. Take time to trust. There are those in the world that prey on the blind trust of others.

There are countless examples of relationships where one partner is charmed by the other, only to discover later that that they have been deceived and the deceiver has perpetrated his or her crime many times before. People often put enormous amounts of faith in others and retain very little faith in themselves. However, it is important to trust ourselves and our intuition about other people in order to understand what our personal truth is.

Evidence of Harry's lack of trust in me showed itself early in our relationship. I just didn't pay attention to it — a shortcoming I have succumbed to in other situations. I have known something at least intuitively if not through hard evidence and still have chosen to ignore the facts. Later I have paid for those lapses of "consciousness" in relationships that have surprised me with their outcomes despite mounting evidence. If I had addressed the evidence at the time I may have, in some cases, saved relationships that were in trouble or ended others when an ending was indicated.

Soon after adopting Harry, I had a dog trainer help me with Harry. When I was teaching Harry how to lie down, Harry did everything in his power to resist. I think he did not trust that something bad would not happen to him. Lying down for any animal that is potential prey for larger animals is a vulnerable position. It takes trust for a dog to lie down, particularly one who has lived by his wits in the street. For Harry, lying down meant trusting that no harm would come to him. I wasn't listening to Harry's fear, his lack of trust in me. How could he trust someone who wasn't listening?

I thought I could convince him of my worthiness by merely loving him. To Harry, love was something that came after trust and respect. Love meant very little to him until he was sure of who I was in relationship to him. This is perhaps totally understood by everyone else in the world, but for me it was a significant learning. With people and now with Harry, I had always led with love and believed that through love fear would dissipate, trust would develop, and respect would be implicit. Harry turned that on its ear. He was interested first in how I dealt with fear, and if I could be trusted, then he would consider whether he would bestow upon me respect and love.

Harry's initial lack of trust and my inability to understand it as such led to a slow decline of our fledgling relationship even before the bite. Harry would not give up a tennis ball to me. He would growl and become more and more menacing. He was suspicious around his food, bones, and other objects he had found. I was told by the dog trainer to take away any bones and all of Harry's tennis balls so that he would not have an opportunity to be possessive. Easier said than done. The more I kept the tennis balls away from him, the more often he found them, even in the most unlikely places. Without his tennis balls, Harry became even more obsessed with them. Harry found tennis balls anywhere and everywhere. He has a similar talent for bones and pizza. I realized that taking away tennis balls wasn't working. I began to see a pattern emerge, and I finally understood that Harry needed to build trust in me.

I began my own program of trust. Instead of taking away all tennis balls from Harry, I gave him one to play with. When he dropped the tennis ball from lack of interest, I scooped it up and lavishly praised him for giving up the ball. Then I would give it back to him. It seemed a little nutty, but it actually began to work. If he growled while he had the ball in his mouth, I would say, "Bad dog," and would go into another room, thereby avoiding a direct confrontational power struggle. He would drop the ball soon after, and I would rush in to scoop it up and put it away. As long as he gave up the ball, he was praised and given back the ball. If he growled, he didn't get the ball back. It got to the point where Harry would pick the ball up from the ground and put it in my hand. I thought, "Cool, I've got this one licked."

Then he attacked me over an oily leather glove he found in a field. He lunged at me growling, leapt up at me and grabbed my sleeve with his teeth, shaking his head with the material in his mouth. I realized then that I had trained him in one context to give something up, but I had not reached the underlying behavior problem — whatever that might be. I lost trust in myself. How could I think I knew better than all the experts who told me the problem with Harry was one of dominance. That my dog didn't respect me, and that I would have to wrest control of my beast or he would wrest control of me.

One day soon after that incident, Harry ran into one of the large beachfront houses, grabbed a container of margarine, and whisked it down to the beach. My frantic calls went unheeded. Harry flipped open the lid and with one large curl of his tongue scooped out a pound of margarine. As I got closer to him, Harry leapt up and raced around the beach triumphantly. I tried to catch him, as if that somehow proved I was being responsible. I knew there was no way I could catch Harry unless he wanted to be caught, which he didn't. He was laughing. He loved to race away and allow me to make a fool of myself in my feeble attempts to catch up to a dog almost as fast as the greyhounds on the beach. It was perfectly clear to me that I had no control of Harry, nor could I trust Harry not to take advantage me.

I began trying out my mishmash of "expert" advice to deal with my aggressive dog. It ultimately led to Harry's confusion and his bite. Harry seemed to be saying, "Enough is enough! Figure this out, lady." Harry's and my role became reversed. Instead of me teaching Harry, Harry was teaching me. If I had trusted myself I might have realized that I had achieved something very special with the tennis ball, and if I had continued to understand Harry's problems as issues of trust, I might eventually have got down to the deeper layers of his mistrust of humans. But I saw only my failure. I heard only my inner critical choral voices raised in a cacophony of self-abuse. You are stupid. You can't train a dog. Your own dog bit you ....

Inner and Outer Voices

WE ALL HAVE MANY inner voices. Learning to distinguish our intuitive inner voice from our critical or destructive inner voice can be life altering. Our critical voices are the ones that put us down, criticize us for our failings, and berate us for not being whatever it is we think we should be: smarter, taller, thinner, prettier, sexier, more athletic, more humorous, quicker witted, the list goes on ad nauseam. I will take more of all of the above please!

Often the critical voices say the things we heard our parents, our teachers, our siblings say when we were younger. "You are so dumb!" "You are so (fill in the blank)!" Sometimes our critical voices are the result of competitiveness. When I was young, I was always at the top of my class, even though I never studied or tried very hard at school. I was a dreamer, losing myself to faraway places in my mind, making the teacher's voice a distant drone. Slowly my position as smartest in the class eroded. I felt devastated but not so devastated that I did anything about it. And because I believed that being smart was a natural inclination, not something that you could work towards and get better at, I decided I was not smart. As a result, after a few years I gave up on myself. I always did well in school and in life, but I held a belief that things come naturally when you are smart and therefore I believed I was not naturally smart.

So, a decision I made about myself in childhood came to shape my entire life for years to come and continues to affect me to this day when I am in a particularly vulnerable state. And so with Harry I was particularly vulnerable — because I measured my acceptability as a human by my troubled relationship with Harry — and my critical voices made mincemeat of my self-esteem. At a certain point, I made a choice to disregard the voices of my past and look to the empirical evidence of the present and what might be possible for the future. Of course, I could turn anything against myself; I could take empirical evidence and say, "My own dog bit me, so we all know what that says about me." But the evidence was that Harry was a problem dog and I, as a first-time dog owner, didn't have the skills to deal with his problems, yet had still managed to teach him to trust me around his tennis balls.

Our critical voices are the voices that leave us unempowered, depressed, or energyless. It is difficult to get out of bed with enthusiasm each morning when you berate yourself at any given moment throughout the day. Think about how hard it is to perform a task when you have a taskmaster hanging over head, haranguing you for not doing it right. It is my critical voice that takes me down and keeps me down. Would you treat a child that way? A dog? Why yourself?

We carry within us the oppressor (the critical voice) and the oppressed (ourselves beaten down). We do not distinguish between the two. As much as we would like to believe that we are wonderfully sensitive people and identify with the oppressed people of the world, most often we identify with the oppressor. We join our internal oppressor and allow that to manage our lives. If we wrote a dialogue of our critical voices, it might go something like:

"You are so stupid."

"Yeah, you're right."

"Absolutely I'm right. You don't deserve (fill in the blank)."

"I feel so bad. I am so stupid."

Dialogues of this type can go on and on in countless variations, with the potential to keep us from being what we can become. Once you begin to engage in dialogue with your internal critic, you begin to see how you have joined forces with it. You might begin trying to talk back so that it sounds something like this:

"You're so stupid."

"If I am so stupid, how did I get to university?"

"Well, you don't deserve it. You got it through luck not intelligence."

"I may not deserve it, but I will try hard."

Did you notice that at the end of the dialogue the oppressor won out, causing the inner voice to accept that you were undeserving? At one time in my life I would have fully agreed with my brutal critical voice and given up. The next step would be to transform the inner critical voice to a kind and loving voice. And the dialogue might go something like this:

"I can't write this essay."

"Take it a little bit at a time."

"I've been trying and I can't do it."

"You've gotten through one section, you can make it through the next."

"I am not so sure."

"You can do this. I know you can. Stay focused. Keep to it."

The dialogue goes on with the second voice supporting and nurturing you rather than haranguing you about how dumb you are.

There is a Native American tale about an elder who tells the story of having two dogs living inside him. One dog is mean and nasty, the other kind and loving. A young warrior asks the elder which dog is winning. The elder replies, "Whichever dog I feed the most." Feed your nurturing side the most. You will find that the burdens from life get lifted, life gets easier for you and those around you.

Some people may have been fortunate enough to be raised in an environment in which emotions were understood, accepted, and reflected back to them. If emotions are consistently ignored or devalued, the world becomes an unresponsive and uncaring place. When a child feels hurt and the parent gives comfort, when a child feels happy and the parent smiles, when a child feels fear and the parent provides safety, the child grows up trusting his or her own responses and trusting that the environment is a loving and caring place: the environment makes sense. From these examples, we can learn how to transform our brutal critics into nurturing voices that pick us up when we are down, empower us when we feel weak, and love us when we feel unloved. We can turn our worlds into kind, loving, and forgiving places.

What happens when others criticize us in life? Learning to accept criticism is a feat in and of itself. We need to learn how to discern what criticism is relevant and what is not. Constructive criticism can teach us a great deal about ourselves, and we can grow from it. On the other hand, criticism that isn't relevant can hurt us. There are many people who, because of their own insecurity, tend to unfairly criticize others. If you find yourself criticizing others, look inwards to locate the source of the pain that leads you constantly to see what is wrong with others. No one is perfect. Once you build self-awareness, you can accept what is not perfect about you, you can accept what is good about you, and you can begin to do the same for others.

By learning how to discern what criticism to accept, you take a giant step towards self-awareness and self-preservation. It is hurtful to accept criticism that is thrust at you when it doesn't have a place in you but is rather a reflection of the person throwing it. On the other hand, accepting relevant criticism can open your mind and be a life-altering experience.

One of my clients initially did not want to accept some feedback she received from a friend. My client believed herself to be thoughtful and kind-hearted, yet her friend said that she was most often self-involved and never seemed to ask or care about how anyone else felt. My client decried how hurtful and mean the comment was, how misunderstood she felt, and how her friend was not much of a friend. I encouraged my client to give an honest and thoughtful analysis of what her friend had said before dismissing the criticism and the friendship outright. My client reluctantly explored the possibility and came upon the awareness that in fact she hadn't paid attention to her friend, that she didn't know what her friend was feeling, and that she wasn't all that concerned with others — only with what they give to her. My client had been aware only of feeling empty and that her friend had not been giving to her.

A deeper exploration led my client to acknowledge the lack of attention and misunderstanding she had felt as a child with her mother. She realized that to this day she looked to all her friends to give her the love and attention that she had craved from her mother, and she blamed them bitterly for not making her feel better. In time, my client grew from the experience, as she felt understood and attended to by me, her therapist, and began showing genuine interest in others and her friend. Their friendship deepened and my client began her first real relationship with a man shortly afterwards. Arthur Ciaramicoli, whose work on empathy I respect, says quite eloquently, "Pay attention to the healing that has come through your relationships rather than focusing on the harm inflicted."

In contrast, I had another client who would become consumed with the criticism of others. He could not differentiate between constructive and destructive criticism. At work he had been promoted to a senior position. When his boss corrected his proposals, his inner critic would paralyze him. He never felt good enough, though he was chosen from many much older and more experienced staffers to be on a senior team. One member of the team criticized him for being too dependent on other members and for not taking charge of a meeting that had led to a discussion of some major issues that had been shuffled aside. My client eventually let go of the criticism as not relevant. He realized he had needed to ask questions from the other team members to get up to speed on the issues. The discussion led by my client inspired the team leader to rethink some of the critical elements in the original proposal. My client also began to accept his boss's corrections for what they were: learning opportunities for creating a powerful proposal, rather than evidence of his inferiority.

How do you handle the criticisms or suggestions from others? Do you become crushed by the weight of thinking that you are imperfect? Do you listen to every critical comment anyone makes and apply it to yourself? Do you negate critical comments when you hear them, believing they couldn't possibly apply to you since you are kind and caring and wonderful and a nice person, damn it! Learn to accept constructive criticism graciously and to see destructive criticism for what it is.

The Intuitive Voice

JUST BEHIND OUR inner critic or parental voice lies our intuitive voice. When I still myself long enough to listen, I can hear it and listen to its message. In the case of Harry, it told me that Harry was worth the time, energy, and knowledge to rehabilitate. My intuitive voice knew there was something I needed to learn in order to reach Harry the way he needed to be reached. As with some of my psychotherapy clients, where an injured soul lurked in the shadows waiting for understanding to come out of hiding and begin to live in the light, Harry was waiting for me to understand him. I needed to listen to him, to hear his heart and soul.

Listening for our intuitive voice is not always easy. We have layers and layers of conscious thought, ideas, opinions, and judgments obfuscating what our true intentions are. We need to stay quiet long enough to truly listen to our hearts, not our minds; to hear what we already know; and to distinguish our critical voice from our intuitive voice. The faintest voice is usually our intuitive voice. It is the one we have learned over the years to silence. It is the one we need to learn to trust.

I have a general rule that helps me distinguish between what my intuitive voice is telling me to do and what my emotions are interjecting. I usually opt for the solution that makes me the most anxious or the most excited, rather than the one that would leave me feeling the most comfortable. That way I always know I am not avoiding an experience I need to have.

Breaches of Trust

IN PSYCHOTHERAPY, TRUST is an issue that often lies at the heart of a client's relationship difficulties. Women and men who have experienced breaches of trust in childhood from their parents have difficulty trusting others. A parent's breach of trust might be the sexual, physical, or verbal abuse of his or her children, or abandonment. Even the death of a parent can be experienced by a young child as a loss of trust in the security of the world: someone that is needed is no longer there to protect, help, and guide.

When parents aren't trustworthy, we lose our first source of learning how to trust our world. Any new relationship is experienced as a composite of every other failed relationship. A parent wasn't trustworthy, so therefore we cannot trust a partner. A former partner wasn't trustworthy, so any new partners will be suspect. A friend betrayed us, so we not only need to proceed with the utmost caution with a new friend but protect ourselves with layers of defenses from the possibility of hurt.

We enter into new relationships encased in armor and then we wonder why we don't have the intimacy that we so deeply desire and need in order to be fulfilled. We carry our past as though it will deliver our future, when what we really need to do is enter every new relationship with hope, openness, and the directness of a child combined with the wisdom of an adult.

Children, when given a solid sense of security from parents, enter relationships, and when they get hurt, they are able to immediately deal with it; they express how they feel, or they fight, or they leave the friendship until they heal and can return to it. If too many unacknowledged hurts accumulate, they end the friendship. Pretty straightforward. As children get older, their experiences build, and they carry those experiences with them — not as wisdom but as a defense. As adults, we enter relationships with our history not just on our backs but carried in front of us and wielded like a sword and shield.

Instead of creating a different way of being, of living into the future we would like, we expect our future to be just like our past and so nothing much ever changes. If we were disappointed once, we live looking for disappointment and sure enough we find it. If we were hurt once, we live looking for hurt and sure enough we find it. If our trust was broken once, we live looking for breaches of trust and sure enough we find it.

Harry found a pizza on the sidewalk once, so he lives looking for pizza on the sidewalk of life and sure enough he finds it. Rarely a day goes by where Harry doesn't find pizza, a tennis ball, or French bread — Harry's favorite things. Harry expects, Harry looks, Harry finds. Harry expected people were untrustworthy, Harry looked at me, and he found a willing partner in me to prove his thesis. We usually think of dogs as living only in the moment, though this is not because they have poor memories. Dogs do learn from the past. They do form habits. They do think, sometimes clearly and sometimes not so clearly. What most dogs do differently than people is to instantly forgive, to live emotionally in the moment.

Broken Bonds

ANYONE WHO HAS discovered his or her partner having an affair can truly understand the devastating effects of a broken trust. For many of us, that trust can never be rebuilt and it marks the end of the relationship. For others, the broken trust is ignored and life goes on but in a crippled manner. Then there are those who choose to try to rebuild the broken bonds of trust and, if successful (it isn't always possible nor always indicated), discover what that can mean in life.

It's horrible to experience a betrayal of trust, but it doesn't necessarily always mean the end of a relationship. There are times when a relationship can be recreated. In a relationship where trust doesn't exist, the relationship will remain plagued until trust is built or the relationship disintegrates. When an individual doesn't trust himself or herself, it is difficult if not impossible to trust another. Trust begins in self-awareness. When we can trust ourselves, we learn how to trust our perceptions of others. When something is wrong, we begin to hear our intuitive voice calling out with discomfort, a sense that something isn't quite as it should be. We begin to see little discrepancies in words and actions, and we pay attention. In time we may discover our discomfort is caused by our own fear of intimacy, and the discrepancies dissipate as we pay closer attention to them. Other times we may discover that our intuition is right on, that our observation skills are developing into something we can trust to deliver vital information about a relationship we are forming.

Betrayal strikes at the heart of the betrayed, at whom they believed they were. Everything gets thrown into question. Who am I, who are you, who was I, who were you, who will I be, and who will you be? When Harry bit me, I was shattered. I questioned my very essence since I believed that dogs always act in sincerity and that dogs know the true intent of people. It never occurred to me that Harry's biting had to do with anything as simple as, "I want that food and you are in the way and no one taught me that I am not allowed to bite when I don't get what I want when I want it." Rather, I led myself on a soul-search that ended up, for all to see, in the form of this book. The short version of what I learned is that sentence. The long version is why that sentence didn't occur to me in the first place.

The Restricted Life

OFTEN, WHEN TRUST becomes an issue, a person's life revolves around creating step-arounds rather than creating lasting solutions. Someone who was abused by his or her parents and so cannot trust others might keep his or her life restricted to maintain a sense of safety or control. He or she might restrict contact with the public by doing a solitary job, put a religious structure around himself or herself, restrict friendships to a few, and perhaps not ever become involved in a romantic partnership. These restrictions allow that person to step around the problem of trust rather than deal with it head on.

Often, when parents don't trust their children to behave properly (quietly, or with restraint, or with dignity and respect) in public places, they do a step-around, restricting their children by not exposing them to restaurants, libraries, or friends' houses. The parents do not necessarily mean harm to their children, they just don't have all the tools with which to teach them. Many children who are difficult to manage have problems beyond the average child and require a greater degree of parenting ability than most of us naturally possess. Getting advice from experts can really help.

A restricted life in dog terms might be one in which the owner doesn't trust the dog to behave off leash, so the dog stays leashed at all times. A dog that cannot be trusted in public must remain confined at home. Confining a dog at home may suffice as a temporary measure only, until the dog can be taught to be a responsible citizen and regain freedom. Many dogs are confined permanently because they are not trusted. They therefore do not lead full lives. A life of strict confinement can eventually lead to more problems. When I eventually went to Adam Stone to learn how to deal with Harry, I was not learning obedience training — which is actually ineffective with most aggressive dogs — I was learning something deeper, what I call "behavioral awareness." Obedience training masks the problem of aggression and does not lead to an ultimately trustworthy pet. A dog that is taught to sit, come, stay, lie down, and heel may be controllable while within the obedience commands, but most dog attacks occur when a dog is not inside a command.

Adam Stone's program is designed to create a deep and lasting bond between the dog and its human. The dog will learn how to think for itself and make good behavioral choices, and the human will learn how to trust that the dog will manage itself with grace and dignity. It is an entirely novel way of approaching dog and human training. Adam supports dogs becoming absolutely trustworthy pets so that they can ultimately attain freedom, including freedom to chose within the confines of safety. I was thrilled to find a way to rebuild a genuine trust between Harry and me.

I met a woman one morning whose dog behaves fine outside but becomes overly protective in her home. Her dog guards her house to the point where she is loath to invite anyone to come to visit. Her dog has pinned one of her friends against a wall. If the dog does allow people into the house and if she raises her hand, the dog will race around the room looking for someone to attack. She has lost so much trust in her dog that she has severely restricted the number of people coming to her home to visit and is considering a life with no visitors at all. Surely, facing the problem squarely by searching out techniques that would allow this woman to rebuild trust in her dog would be a better solution than such a dramatic restriction.

Building Trust by Trusting Yourself

THE SLOW PROCESS OF my building trust with Harry was similar to the building of trust between two people. Trust takes time to develop. The first step towards trusting others, I have come to believe, is to trust yourself. Do you have what is necessary to trust yourself in any given situation? Perhaps you need to learn some new ways to deal with others. For example, by consulting with Adam Stone, I now have the tools to understand and deal with Harry's aggression. I can trust myself to know what to do if I observe Harry's behavior slipping back to his previous ways. I have the tools, and I trust myself not only to know how to use them but to put them into action.

There were many times during Harry's training when Harry

could not be trusted. During training, Harry needed to be regarded not as a house pet but as an untrustworthy dog in training. When he would behave perfectly in several situations, I often would be seduced into believing that Harry was doing well. Then he would surprise me with a snap, a bite, or a growl. Adam says that one of the most common mistakes people make with aggressive dogs is to treat them like house pets during their rehabilitation training time. Rather, the relationship should consistently focus on learning the new way to relate. Similarly, in human relationships we need to consistently use our new tools, continually sharpening our awareness of when we slip back into the old ways.

After the breakup of my marriage, I wasn't sure I trusted myself to create a relationship different than the one I had just come out of. As a consequence, I didn't allow myself to even try a new relationship. It seemed at first as though I couldn't trust someone else with my heart, but what I discovered was that I could not trust myself to be responsible for my own heart. I could not adequately trust that I had the skills to enter into a whole relationship. I needed to learn to trust myself. What that meant for me was trusting that I could look clearly at what the relationship was telling me, and listen to my intuition.

STEP ONE:
BUILDING TRUST BY ACQUIRING SKILLS

Step one to building trust is learning how to trust yourself by acquiring new tools for relating. With my dog, I learned the tools (understanding dogs and pack life, how to correct behaviors) to be a good leader for Harry. For human relationships, any number of tools needs to be learned, depending on the difficulties being addressed. In relationships, we need to identify the areas where we get stuck and learn how to overcome them. You may need to learn how to listen to others. It sounds simple, but most people have no idea how to listen, and true listening makes an incredible difference in a relationship. Listening requires us to stop our own thinking and listen to what someone else is saying without imposing our own prejudices, biases, or agenda onto the speaker. Most often we listen with half an ear, believing that we already know what the speaker is saying. More often than not we are wrong, but we don't realize it because we are busy altering the conversation to fit our own ideas. There are countless books on relationships that suggest excellent tools and countless marriage therapists who can help put a relationship onto a new path.

Step Two:
Building Trust by Paying Attention

"The relationship of trust depends on a state of contact, a contact of my entire being with the one in whom I trust, the relationship of acknowledging depends on an act of acceptance, an acceptance by my entire being of that which I acknowledge to be true," says Martin Buber in *Two Types of Faith*. I think Buber is talking about the interactive aspect of trust. Trust doesn't exist in a vacuum but in the contact made in the relationship.

In learning how to pay attention to the contact point in the relationship, you learn how to observe changes. With Harry, I observe the subtle changes in his behavior that can indicate backsliding. If he flatly refuses to listen to my direction, I consider the best way to respond. I watch for the way Harry greets me, walks with me, approaches other dogs, and communicates with me through his eyes and actions. I pay particular attention to how he listens and responds to me. At this point in our relationship I trust him enough to no longer feel the need to be in strict control of him. Harry is free to wander off when we are in the woods as long as he walks beside me when we are on a city sidewalk.

Similarly in a love relationship, I might pay attention to any changes in the contact, such as distance creeping into communication, sudden or gradual lack of interest, or avoidance of contact. We could respond by talking about what is going on in the relationship, about what the changes might mean. An honest discussion provides more information to evaluate: is this an honest clearing of the air or a continued evasive response that will set our intuition on alert? In a relationship that has attained trust, there is no need to be vigilant, just aware.

Rebuilding Trust

I heard on the radio a fascinating account of rebuilding trust and the capacity for empathy in the animal world. I contacted Dr. Harry Prosen, chair of the Department of Psychiatry with the Medical College of Wisconsin, and talked to him about his work at the Milwaukee Zoo, where he had been invited to assess the behavior of an emotionally disturbed bonobo named Brian. Brian did not trust humans or other primates and exhibited extreme self-destructive behaviors. The reward and punishment system had not worked with Brian. Though Dr. Prosen had never before worked with primates, the zoo team hoped that Dr. Prosen's clinical work with people would help in the creation a program to improve Brian's behavior. The first day Dr. Prosen met the disturbed primate, he narrowly avoided Brian's attempts to throw him and to defecate and urinate on him — an auspicious start. Dr. Prosen asked for a history of Brian.

Brian had been born in a research lab and left in a cage with his abusive father for the first six months of his life, then put in a display cage. Unlike chimpanzees, which come from a patriarchal society, bonobo primates are matriarchal. Females rear their young until they are approximately seven years old; during that time, the offspring may be passed between different bonobo mothers to be loved, groomed, and cuddled. Often the children stay with their mothers up to the age of fourteen years.

Dr. Prosen's treatment program was not unlike Adam Stone's. The first step was to build trust with one person. Dr. Prosen chose Barbara, the head bonobo keeper, a young woman and a mother who had a particularly empathic touch, as the main person to forge the initial human relationship with Brian.

Together, Dr. Prosen and Barbara developed the therapeutic approaches that would be implemented with Brian. The entire team was advised to treat Brian as though he were a young child. Barbara listened, understood, and developed tremendous patience with Brian.

Brian would make great progress, then suddenly and rapidly begin to decline, which was sometimes manifested by bouts of uncontrollable vomiting. Brian was put on a low dose of antidepressant and antianxiety medication to allow Barbara to approach him more easily and to initiate better contact. Brian was also put in a cage with an old and blind female bonobo. The old bonobo slowly took over the patient work of re-mothering Brian. Brian's trust in others and himself built with time, and Brian became a more confident, more social primate.

With the successful treatment of Brian, the zoo gained a reputation for rehabilitating primates. As a result, it received Yuri, a primate that had been hand-raised by humans and went wild with dread when caged with other primates. Upon his arrival, Yuri was placed in the cage with the other primates. Brian went over to Yuri, picked him up, and cuddled him. The zoo team was thrilled to see Brian, a once wild bonobo, make an empathic gesture to the terrified newcomer. They watched the tender Brian give the young primate a coo and a cuddle before handing Yuri over to the mothers to be cared for.

Brian seemed to intuitively understand what Yuri needed. It seemed he had developed empathy and was capable of communicating it. Dr. Prosen came to believe that the bonobos have a well-developed capacity for empathy and perhaps possess an even greater capacity than humans to heal empathic deficits. Dr. Prosen's earlier work had investigated whether empathic deficits in humans could be repaired. He had found that this was extremely difficult in humans, yet in the case of the bonobo Brian, his empathic deficit had been repaired and his capacity for empathy became great. Through his work with Brian, by using empathy, over time, to heal the deep wounds that had been afflicted upon Brian in his early life, Dr. Prosen has added new psychodynamic principles to the usual behavioral approach to animals. Brian was able to trust over time and develop communication and respect that eventually matured into empathy and love.

STEP THREE:
BUILDING TRUST BY TAKING A CHANCE

There comes a point in building trust when it is necessary to take a chance, to stay open and vulnerable and know that you have step one and step two in place. You can trust yourself to know what is going on. You can trust yourself to handle the situation. If you are afraid to be left alone and that is why you don't trust any potential partners, create a support network of friends; discover what it is you are afraid of in being alone and learn about it; take the steps necessary to deal with it. Then, when the opportunity to begin a new relationship comes along, take the chance. Be open to the possibilities.

Taking a chance to trust at times requires a leap of faith. Without that leap there is no possibility of moving forward in your life. Sometimes it may be a mistake, and you find that the trust you afford someone (or your dog) was premature or not deserved. But learn from your mistake, rather than closing down the process entirely. Think about what signs and signals you may have missed, what you may or may not have done to inspire trust from another.

STEP FOUR: LET GO AND PRACTICE TRUST

Therapists often talk about letting go, but how the heck do you do it? First, identify the issue. The issue may be guilt, forgiveness, or obsessing about something traumatic that happened. For months after Harry bit me, I continually recreated the moment of the bite in my imagination. Our minds seem compelled to go over traumatic events in vivid detail as though we might be able to re-do what has happened. It may be that our minds are attempting to recreate the event in slow motion, examining it from one view point then another so that we will perhaps react differently next time. Unfortunately, this activity becomes more like an obsessive rumination than anything constructive. I believe something similar is in operation with guilt and forgiveness. We ruminate about the event that is causing us emotional distress rather than dealing with it. We are hanging on to a problem rather than working towards getting over it.

When something unpleasant happens, we can go over, forever, what we should have done, or could have done, or would have done, if only.... We need to forgive ourselves and move on. We are not perfect and we are awfully arrogant to think that we are not allowed to make mistakes. Learning to tolerate our imperfections, our mistakes, helps us tolerate and forgive others.

One of my clients, though involved with a woman he loved, could not let go of his former wife, despite her affair and their subsequent divorce. He risked losing the woman he loved and he risked losing his peace of mind. He was constantly trying to second-guess what his ex-wife was saying or doing, what she felt, why she did things. He had divorced her, but he had yet to emotionally leave her. It was his bitter resentment that held him in her reluctant arms. Once he understood that it was not her that kept him from moving on but his own anger and resentment that held him hostage, he was able to begin to move on with his own life. He began to see himself as a separate identity, one who saw the world quite differently than did his ex-wife. He also stopped worrying about the differences in how they raised the children (there was no abuse, just different values and philosophies at work) and began forging his own strong relationships with the children.

How to Let Go
Letting go takes practice. There are so many things we hang onto — out of fear and out of our need to maintain control, out of

resentment and bitterness, out of habit or from a lack of trust. Recently former US president Bill Clinton was in Toronto on a speaking tour. He told the audience about his friendship with one of my greatest heroes, Nelson Mandela. Clinton described a private moment with Mandela during which he asked Mandela about being freed after all his years in prison, how he managed not to feel rage and resentment against his oppressors. Mandela replied that of course he felt angry and of course he felt resentment, but the moment he was freed and felt the sunshine on his face, he decided that they had imprisoned him for twenty-seven years and he would not allow them to imprison him for one moment more.

Practicing trust is practicing letting go. Begin with little things. In yoga we learn how to let go of tensing a muscle. It is a step in learning how to let go of other areas of our lives. If you have a tendency to hang onto worry (as I do) as a way of keeping an issue up front and center (as if it isn't anyway!), let it go. I worry constantly about all kinds of things. If it isn't Harry, it's my sister; and if it isn't my sister, it's my nephew; if it isn't my nephew, it's work; if it isn't work, it's a friend; if it isn't a friend, it's this book; if it isn't this book, it's my next one; and so on. Worrying doesn't accomplish anything for any of these things. I have to let go of the worry, or, if it really is something to worry about, I had better get in action and do something about it. If I am worried about Harry, I had better identify the problem, address it, and begin working on it. If I am worried about my deadline, I had better work harder to make sure I meet it.

No Guarantees

I HAVE A YOUNG friend who had never wanted to marry until he was absolutely sure he would know the outcome. He wanted to be sure in advance that the relationship would work. He met a wonderful woman and they were in love. They spent time together and the relationship developed. Their love for each other was palpable, their commitment to each other evident, and their respect for each other manifest. But where was the trust? He didn't want to marry until he felt he could trust himself and his girlfriend to make a lasting marriage. His parents had failed in their attempt and he carried that into his relationship. My friend had difficulty accepting that there are times when one can't be completely certain of the outcome over long periods; there are no guarantees in life. There comes a time when to move forward, you must move with an element of faith. You can do whatever is possible to create the desired outcome, but that outcome is not guaranteed.

Finally my friend got married in Bali in a Balinese ceremony. He and his wife then recreated their ceremony at home for family and friends. It was wonderful to share their special occasion with them and to know that they made their vows with a promise to stay true to their present commitment to love, honor, cherish, and respect each other. Trusting and accepting the uncertainty of the future is an important part of moving forward in life.

Forgive and Forget?

WHEN WE MAKE THE decision to trust, we must acknowledge that sometimes our trust will be betrayed. Therefore, forgiveness is something that we inevitably must talk about when learning how to trust again after a betrayal has occurred.

It is hard to forgive when we feel betrayed, when we can remember in vivid detail the hurts that wound us. Do we just forgive and forget and move on? Anyone who has felt profoundly hurt can attest to the improbability of doing that. But moving on and getting over it is not impossible — it is a process that begins with a first step. Some of us need their hurts to be expressed, heard, and acknowledged. Then, rather than expecting the one who hurt us to make it all better, we must take responsibility for the learning necessary to move past what has traumatized us, without denying it or its impact. Of course, for me, Harry could not do anything about my hurts. I had to heal myself. Some people may think I was crazy to have taken the chance to rehabilitate him, but it has ended up being worth it. I made the decision to rebuild the trust with Harry, gained the new knowledge I needed to trust myself in the process, and took a chance that I could create a different outcome through my new learning. Working through this with Harry helped me gain new insights into some of the trust issues in my human relationships.

According to the I Ching, "The event is not important, but our response to the event is everything." We tend to think of forgiveness as a feeling, a feeling that has its own existence within us, beyond our conscious control. However, it is more useful to think of forgiveness as a choice. It is one that cannot be made until the processing of the hurt or betrayal is done, but it is a choice nevertheless. Choosing to forgive is not about condoning the hurtful actions of another, but it is what we need in order to move on from the experience. By letting go, we are able to move on to the future without forgetting or suppressing the past traumatic events. Often there is no closure with serious traumas, but this is not to say that they do not fade with time. Each day we wake up and begin our day anew, our choices for the day ahead of us. We can choose to move on with our lives or not.

Not forgiving can involve blaming ourselves or blaming others. If we have been hurt by someone and wallow in self-blame ("If I had only done this or that; If I hadn't done this; If I had said that; If I had been better, funnier, prettier, smarter"), we are stuck and won't be moving ahead in life. Humans tend to hold on to hurts to hold on to what is constant, what is known, what doesn't lead us into unknown territory. If we move on from self-blame, we are taking responsibility for our lives, taking our rightful place in the world of action. When we blame ourselves, we feel we have no right to our feelings. We need to claim that right for ourselves because no one else in the world will do it for us.

If we instead blame others for what befalls us, we are again not taking responsibility for our lives. We give over our lives to others to make or break our happiness or success. When we forgive ourselves or others by releasing ourselves from inaction and moving into action, we become free from the past. That is when new possibilities arise. When we have taken the time to let go of the past, learn the tools necessary to trust ourselves, prepare ourselves for a new possibility, and embrace the journey, forgiveness is achieved.

Closed Doors and Open Windows

I HAVE ONE FRIEND who says she doesn't trust anyone. She begins from the assumption that others are not to be trusted, and she never lets her doors and windows open wide enough to discover whether or not a particular person is trustworthy. Our friendship is limited by the lack of trust; it also acts as a barrier to love. Perhaps that is what she wants to protect herself from. Needless to say, she has never been in a long-term relationship and suffers from a profound sense of disappointment with people.

I have another friend who trusts indiscriminately in her relationships with men, though not in any other aspect of her life. When involved with a man, she doesn't pay attention to the contact point of the relationship, is always shocked by how her relationships seem to end suddenly, and is shocked by the signs she failed to notice along the usually short journey.

Both these women have situated the trust outside themselves. One walks through life with all her doors closed, the other as though she has no doors. Both these states are dangerous. They both allow the power to reside in the other person.

Healthy Trust

I HAD A CONVERSATION with Tova's mother (my dear friend whose dog is one of Harry's girlfriends) one day about trust. She said that when she was young, she always trusted she could reach out to someone for help and that belief gave her the confidence to go out in to the world. She is observing her teenage daughter developing in a similar way. Paul Ferrini writes in *Silence of the Heart*, "Stop imposing your expectations on the events and circumstances of your life. Just let life unfold and see what happens." Our attempts to control outcomes are at the very least conducted in vain. At worst, expectations generate disappointments, and disappointments generate anger. All we can do is pay attention to the signs and trust that we will know how to react.

When Harry is at risk for biting, there are signs along the way to which I need to pay attention: Harry stops listening to me and begins to strike out on his own; he carries his head and tail in an arrogant manner; he starts posturing with another dog or mounting another dog during play for dominance. If I allow this behavior to continue, soon enough his responses to commands become sloppier and sloppier.

In our human relationships, the signs are different but they are there nevertheless. With a love partner, we must pay attention to changes in behavior, changes in attention, and changes in our partner's appearance. Though such changes don't necessarily mean that something untoward is happening, they can be indicators that we need to pay attention to our partner. When we don't pay attention to changes, trouble can come calling. Sometimes it is too late, but sometimes it is just in time. When we don't pay attention, we lose our ability to make good choices for ourselves.

We spend time every day understanding others, intuiting what others think and feel, imagining what others might need or want. Those same skills can go towards telling us whom, when, and how we can trust. We must reserve some objectivity so that we see the world the way it really is, not the way we want it to be. "Empathy can help us sense danger. It can let us see into the hearts and minds of people who intend to deceive, manipulate, or harm us," writes Arthur Ciaramicoli in *The Power of Empathy*.

Humans and Animals Trust Differently

ANIMALS ARE ALWAYS paying attention to the subtlest signs in others to take cues as to how to behave. Elizabeth Marshall Thomas, writer of *The Social Lives of Dogs*, says, "To be sure, most animals are better at empathetic observation than we are, not only because they are more aware of small details, but also because they credit the evidence of their senses. We don't, or not nearly as much, so we miss most of what animals notice." We have come to rely on words to deliver what could be common gut responses. Our words are not necessarily the sharpest tools of communication. Think of how often we misinterpret one another or twist meanings to suit our own purposes or use words inaccurately. Dogs, on the other hand, constantly communicate with one another, through subtle and not so subtle signs. They use their ears, tails, hackles, lips, eyes, and body movements to convey a full range of emotions and expressions. They combine their expressions in a variety of contexts that are understood among canines.

An example of how humans bandy about terms without necessarily sharing a common definition occurred one day with a group of dog friends. We spent countless hours discussing what we meant by dominant behavior, then went through a similar exercise with the idea of weak leadership. It was fun to be challenged in fundamental ways, to really think out what we meant by those terms. But what it really did was highlight how we often don't have the common understanding of words we think we do. What I meant by dominant was slightly different from what

Jennifer meant and was different again from how Judy thought about it, and so on.

My beginning to stand between Harry and other dogs that were harassing him was an essential building block in the process of Harry coming to trust me. Harry seemed to immediately understand that I was protecting him, that I was becoming a leader. Since then, Harry comes to me for direction whenever he is uncertain. He knows I will restrict him from behaving badly and protect him when others behave badly towards him. We built trust around food by keeping a huge pail of food filled to the top so that he never feels deprived of sustenance. Harry understands that if he gives, he gets. Dealing with all these issues enhanced our relationship. Harry now trusts me to tend his wounds, clip his toenails, give him medicine, and clean his ears.

What Harry makes obvious to me is the transient quality of his trust. It is never blind. His trust depends on what I am doing at the moment. One day he may trust me completely, the next I have done something, allowed some nuanced sign to reveal a vulnerability in me, and Harry decides he will take care of himself, thank you very much. Eventually Harry's trust of me will not be so context-specific, but it will evolve over time. Once he realizes that most of the time I am trustworthy, rather than just occasionally, I will not have to be so vigilant about his behavior and will allow small infractions. We are in the process of that with each other now. At one time, I was on top of Harry for any behavior that even hinted at dominance. Now I allow some small things to slip by. Harry looks at me at those times and seems to smile as if to say, "Hmm. You've learned well, grasshopper. I didn't have my heart in that growl; I just wanted to see how you would react." No; now I must really understand the nuances of our interactions and react appropriately.

Resistance and Persistence

THE LESSON FOR A dog to crawl is a subtle lesson meant to reveal the resistance in our dogs, since if resistance exists in one area, it is likely to reside in others. And so it does with both our dogs and ourselves. Teaching the dog to crawl without food treats or without a table to force the dog to stay in a crouching position is partially about teaching our dog to trust that no matter what we ask, we are not being unreasonable in our demands. Of course, that requires us not to be unreasonable in our demands of our dogs. If we did ask them to do something that was dangerous to them or that they could not possibly do, we would indeed lose their trust. Our dogs need to learn that we will ask them to do only something that is safe for them to perform. They need to know that their human will not ask anything more than that which they are capable of.

Charles Eisenmann talks a great deal about asking his dog, London, the original Littlest Hobo, to perform difficult feats but never anything impossible or unsafe. After years of working together, London would never second-guess Eisenmann — until one day when London realized the pile of boxes he was supposed to jump from was unsafe. When London resisted, Eisenmann thought the dog was being stubborn, but then, trusting London's combination of thinking ability and trust of his owner, realized something must be wrong. Eisenmann checked the pile and discovered it was unsafe. This is the complexity of thinking that we hope to come close to developing with our dogs.

Soon we will have trained our dogs to think on a level at which they just know how to be dignified, self-correcting dogs. Our dogs will no longer engage in foolishness. Our dogs will become like Charles Eisenmann's amazing Littlest Hobo dogs. They may not perform as skilfully as Eisenmann's dogs, but they will have traversed an incredible journey from aggressive dog destined for execution to trustworthy pet. And we will have developed our own style of dealing with our challenging dogs.

Some dog trainers and dog enthusiasts have questioned the veracity of Harry's rehabilitation. They find it hard to believe that an aggressive dog has been transformed the way I have described Harry's transformation. But Harry always possessed a stable temperament and that likely contributed to the success of his rehabilitation. Where once Harry was a dog who bit, now Harry is a loving, trustworthy pet. I have observed the transformation of other aggressive dogs, but I could not in all honesty say that all aggressive dogs are capable of being rehabilitated. I am not an aggression expert, nor much of a dog expert for that matter. I have learned a great deal about dogs and dog behavior, but I can hardly consider myself an expert after owning and training only one dog. But in observing many aggressive dogs and their owners, I have seen some owners end the training prematurely, for a variety of reasons. I don't know the outcome for these dogs. Some may have flourished in different training environments. The dogs and owners I have seen who have stayed the difficult course of Adam Stone's training program have emerged with the most wonderful pets and an extraordinary amount of dog knowledge as a result.

To Trust Is to Give

WHEN HARRY AND I are in tune with each other, we can both relax. Life becomes not just coping with a problem dog but a real joy with genuine communication. There is no longer any need to control behavior, to be hypervigilant in order to anticipate problems. There is trust. It is an extremely gratifying place to be in a relationship and it allows life to become far richer. When problems arise, we can deal with them with a knowing that we will return to a balanced state.

Trust is elemental to developing intimacy. Where trust has

been established, intimacy grows and true giving occurs. Communication is most often clearer between people who trust each other; there is no perceived need to protect the self from the other. In the initial stages of a romantic relationship, many people feel they must hide their true intentions until they sense their intentions will be reciprocated. Spouses discover that a deeper honesty is possible with trust. When trust exists between parents and teenagers, parents do not experience the need to exert control; they trust that their children will behave within reason. Conversely, when teenagers trust their parents, they feel that they can come to their parents with any problems they might have, rather than having to hide what they are going through.

When Harry and I achieved a trusting relationship, our life together transformed from one of tension, suspicion, and misunderstanding into one of joy, love, and great fun. Now there are days at the beach when Harry races around by himself with what seems like a big smile on his face. At one time, Harry needed another dog to play with, a squirrel to chase, or a ball to retrieve. Now he seems to be a very happy, confident, and comfortable dog. We genuinely enjoy each other and it is wonderful not to feel the tension of fear and stress that at one time regularly plagued our life together.

Building trust with Harry gave me a deep appreciation of the role trust plays in all our relationships. Discovering trust within a relationship can be an extremely freeing experience. With deep trust, one gains the confidence to freely give to another without fear, inhibitions, or regrets.

Discovering a Richer Life Through Trust

LEARNING TO TRUST is a process that takes time. Broken trust hurts, and as intelligent creatures, we tend to avoid situations that have caused us pain in the past. However, the situations we tend to avoid are not necessarily the ones we should avoid. Each new relationship has the potential to be something different when you learn from past experience.

It takes time to build trust, and time to heal a broken trust. Learning how to leave the past behind and live into the future brings freedom to a life worth living. It is essential for the wholeness of relationships that we develop the ability to listen to our inner voice, discern the voices of others, release old ideas that no longer serve us, and begin to trust ourselves. The processes of building trust with Harry has deepened my appreciation of forgiveness and trust as a central theme of the journey towards a richer life.

LESSONS IN TRUST

- Stay in touch with your intuition and respond to your inner critic with positive messages to yourself.
- Feed your nurturing side.
- Accept constructive criticism and disregard destructive criticism.
- Choose the solutions that make you less comfortable; they challenge you more.
- Gain new skills to deal with difficult people and issues and trust yourself to use them.
- Pay attention to changes in contact with your partner and friends as an early-warning signal system.
- Take a chance.
- Practice trust and pay attention to the outcome.
- Accept that there are no guarantees.
- Forgive so that you can move past painful betrayals that hold you back from engaging fully in your life.
- Create an environment in which trust can be built.
- Enjoy the intimacy that develops from trusting.

Harry on Respect:
Honor Yourself and Others

The truth that makes men free is for the most
part the truth which men prefer not to hear.

— H. AGAR

L IVING WITH HARRY WAS like living with an extremely
difficult partner or a child with ADHD (attention deficit
hyperactivity disorder). I had to constantly define and redefine my
personal boundaries lest I become "eaten up." I allowed it to happen in my first marriage. I knew better in my second, though it
still happened. It took Harry and his extremely sharp teeth to
make the point. When it came to self-respect, I was deficient.

There is an old saying, "You teach others how you want to be
treated." I have also heard it said in this way: "You get what you
tolerate." Both these sayings are filled with great wisdom. If you
tolerate being badgered by someone then you will be badgered.
If you tolerate doing all the household chores then you will end
up doing all the chores. If your partner treats you without
respect then you have not adequately taught your partner how
you wish to be treated.

The truth in the sayings became painfully clear when I thought about them in terms of Harry and me. I had been tolerating his manipulations. I had been tolerating his aggressiveness. I had been giving Harry the fruits of love, warmth, and caring without requiring Harry to be respectful. Harry certainly taught me how he wanted to be treated, but I had not taught him. Once again, I found myself in a one-sided relationship.

Never again! I finally get exactly what those sayings mean. Not just intellectually, but viscerally. After the ultimate in disrespect — from a dog no less — I finally understood what respect is all about. It is not about giving. It is not about loving. It is not about understanding. It is about feeling yourself worthwhile. It is about valuing yourself and others. It is about being responsible for yourself and accountable to others. It is about concern. It is a deep reverence for all life, including your own. I grew to truly understand that operating from a core of respect for yourself and others is a cornerstone to living more fully.

I was mostly raised by my grandmother, a self-sacrificing, fine, religious woman who dedicated herself to the service of others. My grandmother commanded respect by the mere virtue of her presence. She was an extremely strong woman, very generous of spirit, kind, loving, and caring, yet she had powerful boundaries. Somehow my grandmother seemed to be a lot better at life than I. I had lost something in the translation of this lesson from strong adult woman to small child. I thought I had embraced my grandmother's values, but I had somehow left myself out of the equation.

In my propensity for self-criticism I made myself not count in my own world. I waited for someone to do it for me, for someone to give me respect, instead of insisting on it for myself. Dr. Phillip McGraw on the *Oprah Winfrey Show* once said emphatically to a woman who was going along with what her husband wanted at the expense of her own desires, "If you don't claim it for yourself, no one else will!"

The walls of my grandmother's house were covered with wise sayings in pictures and on plaques. "I complained I had no shoes, until I met a man who had no feet." "Do unto others as you would have others do unto you." "You can't till the soil by turning it over in your mind." To this day I conjure the image of her walls and the wisdom they imparted to me. I have never been much of a complainer, and I am sure it is the impact of the man with no feet on an impressionable young child. When I do complain, I become aware of it very quickly and I immediately try to do something about the problem. Being a problem solver is one of my strengths, but a result of not being a complainer has been to not speak up for my own needs. Harry forced me to think hard about what I needed and deserved from my dog, and as a result, from other people. I have had to develop respect for my own needs.

Who Is to Blame?

THERE ARE THOSE who immediately accept all the blame for problems in life and then there are those who feel the rest of the world is at fault. Often these types of people find each other. I tend to be of the former category. In my case, Harry's behavior was the problem, and as long as I was looking within only myself, I wasn't seeing the true source of the problem and therefore I was not dealing with it. To do that I had to look outwards. I had to see what was there in the real Harry, not in the ideal Harry.

If you think you are the problem, chances are you are unlikely to believe that you can solve the problem. It matters most where you are focusing your attention. It is as simple and as difficult as that. Once I began to focus on what was out there — the unwanted behaviors that were disrespectful to me — I became clear as to how I wanted to live in my life. Not just in relationship to Harry but with the whole world. I definitely did not want to struggle with a dog ad nauseam, and I did not want to maintain people in my life who were inconsiderate of me. Wow! I suddenly felt so clear and so free. Years of struggling with *who I am* suddenly melted into *who they were being.*

A wise friend once said to me, "When you know who you are, Cindy, you will know who others are." At first I felt frustrated because I didn't know who I was and I didn't know how to figure it out. But by paying attention to what was happening in my relationships with others, it began to make sense. It felt profound. His words initiated a journey, one that paved the way for a whole new understanding of respect and reverence.

On the other hand, if you always feel that everyone else is the problem in your life and they are the reason you are unhappy/poor/alone/fill-in-the-blank, you have some serious soul searching to do. Blaming others for your life is not empowering. It puts the power for change in others rather than where it needs to begin, which is in yourself. This doesn't mean that if you are unhappy because you always do the dishes, you must always do the dishes and be happy about it. That is a peace-at-any-price solution. It means that if you are unhappy, do something about it. You need to take responsibility for how you feel and what you are allowing to take place in your life. Talk to whoever is leaving his or her dishes for you and let that person know how you feel and what can be done. You might want him or her to share equally the responsibility for dishes, or that person might come up with an even better plan than the one you thought of, so stay open to suggestions. The possibilities are endless once you begin to approach problems in a respectful way. The effort it takes to see a problem clearly rather than automatically blaming yourself or someone else is worthwhile because you are then open to genuine solutions.

One client of mine, Lauren, a bright and energetic woman, lamented to me that she wished her boss would accept some responsibility for having made her life at her job miserable. After one year at her job, she had gone from being enthusiastic to frustrated, angry, and spiraling into depression. At work Lauren felt unappreciated and disrespected, and felt she had no authority to implement her ideas. She wanted to accomplish things, yet felt she could do nothing to please her boss. These were all feelings Lauren could recall experiencing with her father. This situation was an opportunity for Lauren to learn to overcome the feelings that keep her stuck needing the validation of an authority figure.

Lauren felt strongly that it was unfair her boss didn't have to change when it was his behavior that had caused her problem. Lauren thought that if only he would listen to her ideas and allow her to implement them, he would see that the programs she developed for the company were great. Through our discussion, she began to accept that, unfortunately, life is often not fair and there are people who refuse to take responsibility for their actions. She began to understand that she could either continue to lament the unfairness of it all or decide to take action to leave the situation, avoid the situation, alter the situation, or change her behavior and responses. Since it was not a good time for Lauren to look for another job, she was left with changing how she handled the situation.

Although Lauren had initially wanted to prove her self worth to her boss and was therefore vulnerable to his approval or lack of it, once she shifted her attention away from proving herself and into doing what could be done within the context and limitations of the position, she became able to tolerate it until she could find another job. She also discovered the freedom to work without the need for outside validation. By practicing the four cornerstones, Lauren gained an awareness of what was possible and what was not within this context. She decided that she would communicate courageously with her boss, knowing it wouldn't get her anywhere, but at least she would know she had done everything in her power to maximize the possibility of accomplishing her goals. She learned to trust her intuition and build a stronger sense of herself as a worthy and capable person. She respected herself knowing that she was capable of more and so began looking for a position elsewhere that might satisfy her ambitions. She respected her boss's unconscious decision to never change the status quo of the organization even though he stated otherwise at every opportunity. Lauren learned to feel good and valuable within herself and to not rely on someone else to make her feel that way.

I have often observed people who are rehabilitating their aggressive dogs not paying attention to what else is going on in their lives. Frequently, respect issues are coming up in their human relationships as well, in one form or another. One woman had started boundary training with her aggressive dog, Jewel, after Jewel had bitten one of her children in the face. The woman complained that her boyfriend would allow Jewel out of the crate before the dog's allotted time was up, and her brother would tell her that the training program was unnecessary since if she just smacked Jewel across the muzzle, the dog would stop biting. The boyfriend and her brother were both living with her in her tiny house without paying rent, while she was barely making ends meet.

This woman was being disrespected by everyone and her dog! When she tried to get respect from Jewel, her boyfriend and brother undermined her every effort. Think of what her child must feel, knowing that he had been bitten and no one was taking it seriously enough to make certain it would never happen again. The woman felt helpless to stand up to her boyfriend and her brother. She felt helpless to effect any change in Jewel's behavior, yet she was unwilling to find another home for the dog. Though the solution to her problem may seem totally clear to us, the woman lived shrouded in delusions, blaming everyone else for her lack of success.

I do not know how this story ultimately turned out. I only hope that the woman gained the strength she needed to alter the course of events that seemed destined to unfold. Only by recognizing that she deserved respectful behavior from the men in her life as well as her dog could she take the steps necessary to transform her difficulties and protect her child. Learning to respect herself would be the start. This would allow her to set new boundaries with her housemates and with her dog.

Free Will

HUMAN BEINGS HAVE the capability of consciousness, of self-reflection, and of determining our own behavior. We are not robots, though we often act as though we were, allowing knee-jerk reactions to determine our actions without consideration of the consequences.

Most difficulties revolve around our choices. Sometimes when faced with a problem we feel that we have no choice but to react in a certain prescribed manner or that we have to react the way we always have, the way our therapist said we should, the way our friend suggested, or the way our mother or father reacted. Often these automatic responses come from our feelings of self-blame or blaming others, and they only reinforce unhelpful patterns in our relationships. The reality is that when we step back for a moment and engage our conscious thinking and strategic skills, we realize that with a little practice in opening our minds, we have many choices in the way we react. Such a thoughtful, strategic reaction is more likely to be respectful of yourself and others and produce more positive results.

Harry is a wonderful teacher for this. He provides me with countless opportunities to react to him. Each time Harry did what he did because that was what Harry did, I had an opportunity to slow down, think, and choose how to react. That does not mean I should deny instinctive reactions, but rather that I should choose when and where and how to react. Often with an aggressive dog you have only a fraction of a second to decide how to react. Your dog sees another dog approaching. That dog raises his hackles (his hair stands on end!), your dog stiffens, you may even feel a vibration through the leash (yes, that was him growling!), and pow, the other dog leaps onto your dog (it is always someone else's fault!), and your dog responds instantly to the challenge.

By planning and practicing my responses to a variety of situations, I have been able to teach Harry to respond differently. Where Harry once treated every sidewalk as his personal territory to be defended to the death whenever another dog had the audacity to approach him, he now rarely gives a second glance at a passing dog. Sometimes he wants to greet them, have a quick sniff, and move on. Sometimes he wants me to walk interference and he will maneuver himself so that he will have me walking past the other dog. Sometimes he walks a wide arc to avoid the dog. These are all new behaviors he thinks about and chooses. Now, think of this. If it is possible to teach a dog to slow down his mental processes to react differently to a threat, perceived or otherwise, do you think that a human's vastly more developed brain might be capable of the same reengineering? I believe so.

There are times when we all appropriately choose to react to something with anger and other times we choose to react with understanding. There are still other times when our automatic responses kick in and we respond without choice, without freedom. We "make nice" when we wish we hadn't, or we make a snide comment when kindness would have made all the difference. We need to stop long enough to check our sometimes destructive automatic responses, yet still be in close enough touch with our instinctual gut responses when we need them. Still, when events that challenge us present themselves, we can always try to ask ourselves, "What do I want to do here? What would a wise person do? How will the other person feel after I say or do 'x'? How will I feel? Am I reacting through habit or choice?"

Through my work, I have read about philosopher Michel Foucault's conception of freedom, which I understand to be the space in which to reinvent yourself; you have that freedom to the extent to which you create that space. Many of us need to work at creating the space to rethink our reactions and thereby exercise our freedom to reinvent more powerful selves.

Harry entered my life with no natural deference to humans. He really didn't care too much for humans. If they fed him, great; if they patted him when he wanted, great; if they got in his way, too bad for them. He is a wily beast and learned quickly how to play to my weaknesses and avoid my strengths. When he gave the pathetic, feel-sorry-for-me eyes or curled his lips and gave his evil eye, I unwittingly complied with Harry's behavior modification program of me by giving what he wanted. By not thinking clearly about what was happening, I got caught up in the sense of crisis, of having to put out a fire, instead of taking the time to calmly come up with a plan to safely deal with his aggression and ulti-mately change his behavior.

One day Harry had his head thrust deep inside a garbage can. I yelled at him to get out. Harry came out with half a chicken car-cass in his mouth. He glared at me darkly as though daring me to take the bones out of his mouth. I panicked and helplessly demanded that he drop it. I was worried that he would eat the chicken bones and they would get lodged somewhere where they weren't supposed to get lodged and he would get sick and die. Likewise, I was worried that if I approached him, he would drop the chicken carcass and latch onto my bones instead. I yelled and yelled to no avail. Finally I turned and walked away home. He dropped the carcass and came running after me. He spent quite a few hours in his crate after that.

On this occasion, rather than following the advice of many obe-dience dog trainers who teach that you must catch the dog in the act and correct the behavior within seconds so that the dog will understand what he is in trouble for, I followed Adam Stone's teaching that you can say to your dog, "I see what you are doing. I don't like it. And since you are not listening to me right now, you will go into your kennel when you get home." I can attest to the fact that this works. Many people cannot believe that Harry understands what he is going into his kennel for, and I really don't know exactly what he understands. I just know that, behaviorally, Harry corrects himself the next time the situation arises.

Another day, while on the beach before dawn practicing ba gua chang, a martial art much like tai chi that cultivates and uses inner chi (energy), Harry ran around barking at people walking on the boardwalk in the early morning darkness. It was awful. At first I frantically called Harry to come to me, to stop barking, to get in the car, to get anywhere but where he was. Harry just danced around the beach, eluding me and laughing at my ineptness. When I caught myself reacting wildly, I decided I would temporarily disown my barking, disobedient dog and return to my practice. A few minutes later, Harry stopped barking at people, most likely because he wasn't getting a reaction from me, and he started coming closer to where I was "walking the circle," an integral ba gua chang practice. When one of my teachers, James, and I went to sit on the beach for our sunrise meditation, Harry sat by my side and waited for us to finish. Only once did he go up to James to lick his face to try to get a reaction.

Harry is always Harry, though at times I wish he were more like my friend Jennifer's dog, Buddy, a dignified and gentle giant. Sometimes I struggle with accepting Harry for who he is. He is often goofy and silly, which drives me crazy, but I am really grateful that he has become a wonderfully loving animal that no longer feels the need to intimidate and threaten humans to get what he wants.

Discover Life Lessons in Current Circumstances

IT WAS THROUGH looking at my current circumstances that I learned the life lessons that had held me back in countless situations. The guru with his straggly beard taught me to look at what was going on existentially in our life together to learn about myself. If we all begin to approach our own lives with that mindset, we will be closer to finding our own solutions. We must pay attention to what our lives and our relationships are telling us about ourselves. If everyone is angry with us, we might be angry. Let's be honest. If we constantly feel taken advantage of, either we have not provided sufficient boundaries for ourselves or we do not recognize the generosity of others. This will be discussed in full later in this chapter. It is really important to develop our awareness of what patterns emerge in our lives and how we can use that awareness to develop ourselves. I have my guru, hooligan Harry; you might have your mate, your teenager, your next-door neighbor, your boss, your parakeet, or your parents. You may even find your lessons in an inanimate object.

As an interesting example of the latter, Fritz Perls, the father of Gestalt therapy, told a wonderful story about a violinist who came to see him because his fingers were going numb and he was at risk of losing his position as First Violin in the symphony. The violinist had already spent countless years in psychoanalysis when he first noticed the tingling in his fingers and believed the symptom to be of an emotional origin. The man arrived for his first visit. Fritz Perls invited him in, asked him about his fingers, and then asked him to play something on the violin for him. The violinist replied that he had not brought his violin. He said he had never before been asked to play in therapy, just to talk about his past. Perls asked him to stand as though he were playing and pretend he had his violin.

The man stood up and began playing his absent instrument. Perls immediately noticed that the man stood with his feet tightly closed together in a ballet-style third-position, one heel fitted into the arch of the other foot, his back then tilted forward, and his shoulder muscles pinched into his neck. Perls had the man adopt a wider stance. Immediately his back straightened and his shoulders relaxed, releasing his neck muscles and liberating the blood flow to his fingers. The man had not given himself a solid foundation. By clearly looking at the issue for what it was, Perls very quickly got to the bottom of the dilemma.

Boundary Training

BOUNDARY TRAINING FOR dogs is an important part of gaining the respect of your dog. Establishing boundaries is also a profound learning experience for human relationships. Most difficulties in relationships arise when boundaries are either not clearly established, constantly encroached on, or rigidly upheld. Since my troubled relationship with Harry came to light, I have spent a great deal of time observing the personal boundaries or personal space of people. Some people carve out their space and as though invisible shields were in operation — no person, child, nor animal dare enter close to them. Then there are those who welcome trusted people into their space. These people seem open but not necessarily vulnerable. And there are those who seem to have no control over who enters their personal space. I suspect these are people who grew up in households where respect was probably in deficient supply.

Adam Stone tells a story about being in Australia studying dingo dogs. He claims that it was in watching a dingo bitch handle her puppies that he created part of his program of respect, boundary training. He watched the dingo bitch allow her calm puppies to wander off and come back to her, but her overly exuberant puppies were constantly picked up by the scruff of their neck and taken back inside an invisible boundary close to where she was.

It is a major part of Adam Stone's training program for aggressive dogs. We create a boundary and the dog must learn to respect it. There is no door to the boundary; the dog must stay behind the boundary merely because we have asked it to. Because there is no closed door marking the boundary, the dog learns to think about where he is allowed to be, or not be. In the wild, there is no door marking the territory of a pack, yet wolves and wild dogs can discern where they should be and where they shouldn't be. This is the genesis of respect.

The boundary is wonderfully transportable once learned. I can take Harry into a new environment and in just five to fifteen minutes he will completely understand where he can and cannot go. At my friend Evelyn's house, Harry learned in two minutes to stay in her kitchen. However, after a few hours, Harry, always testing limits, broke the boundary to race upstairs to her spare room, grab a stuffed toy, and run back downstairs to show us his prize. It was a stuffed conch shell with a removable stuffed crab inside. We couldn't help but laugh at Harry's continued audacity and his choice of stuffed toy.

At the cottage I rented this summer with my sister, my brother-in-law, my nephew, Maxx, and his friend, Reid, Harry was boundaried in my bedroom during dinner and at various other times during our holiday. He was still in training at this point in our life together. Harry would sometimes come to the open French doors and try to tempt the others to give him the okay to come out, but I had asked everyone to strictly comply with my wishes for him to stay in my bedroom until I gave the okay. At first, Harry would lie down at the invisible boundary with his nose and his toes just crossing the threshold. Adam calls that fencing. It shows that the dog has not completely given up his hope to be allowed out of the room. Later, Harry resigned himself to the room and curled up in the corner. Harry's behavior the rest of the cottage stay was impeccable. He listened, he was calm and respectful of everyone, and he did not run into other people's yards when he was outside off leash.

The technique of boundary training is quite simple. You define your boundary in your house first. It can be a room or it can be in the middle of the room. There does not have to be door or a concrete divide. You leave the dog's leash on, put the dog behind the boundary, and say something like, "Out," "Get out," "Leave," or another word you choose to indicate what you want. Each time the dog leaves the boundary (you want him to leave so you can teach him the boundary), pick up the leash and take him back inside the boundary. You can say the words again or you can say nothing at all. Once he has learned the boundary, introduce distractions. Roll a ball out of the boundary into the no-go zone. Have a person or another dog walk by. Ring the doorbell. The boundary, when properly taught, can fix a multitude of behavior problems, is convenient when you need your dog to stay out of your space, and defines leadership. Your dog becomes more respectful of you.

The boundary is not a punitive place. It shouldn't be doggy hell, just a place you tell your dog to go to because you want him to be there for whatever reason or no reason. It is when you send your dog to a boundary place for no reason that real learning begins to take shape inside the dog.

Find Your Center, Not Your Balance

ONE DAY WHILE walking downtown with Alex, my ba gua teacher, he told me a wonderful story about martial arts that one of his teachers had told him. The essence of the story was, "Find your center, not your balance." If you try to keep your balance, you will be thrown off if you step on a pebble or a twig, but if you locate your center and maintain it, being thrown off balance won't matter because you will return to your center. Kind of like a gyroscope that always locates its center no matter what is happening to its balance. Though we were deep in discussion about martial arts practice, this is a perfect metaphor for relationships. There will always be things to throw you or your partner off balance, but if you can find and retain your center, you can right yourself no matter what has happened and continue through life with grace and equanimity.

When I had problems with Harry, I had treated him like my sun, my moon, and my stars. I think Harry thought he was the most magnificent beast in the universe. He was not. I have noticed this pattern in my love relationships as well. I have often created relationships in which there was an imbalance because I had, in a way, located my center inside the center of my partner. I paid more attention to what my partner wanted, felt, and experienced than what I wanted, felt, or experienced. Using the four cornerstones now helps me maintain my center. I pay attention to what I am experiencing and I communicate openly what I need or want. I trust myself and pay attention to the contact being made, and I respect the relationship. This doesn't necessarily mean the relationship will stay together, but it does mean that I will feel that I have lived wholly and completely within that relationship as much as is presently possible. Our ability to be honest with ourselves and know ourselves grows with practice and experience. Keeping centered in a relationship requires you to honestly know your feelings and your experiences and to be wholly responsible for them.

If you want something to be different in a relationship, you must make it known how you want it to be different. If you make your desires known and if nothing changes, it is time to ask yourself some important questions. Is this something that will take time to change? Something that will never change and that you cannot live with? Or perhaps something that will never change but that you can accept because of all the great aspects of your relationship?

You need to take the time to evaluate with love in your heart and reality in your mind. Are you accepting something that will eat away at the fabric of your self-respect? Or are you accepting something that in the overall picture is not that important? Do you feel respected by your partner? Do you respect your partner? There is no need to begin refusing to be generous to your partner just because you've read this and think you have to be selfish. It is when your generosity comes at the expense of your self-respect that you may want to reevaluate the foundation of your relationship. Are you standing on a tight base with pinched nerves or are you on comfortable footing?

If you have been tolerating something you dislike for many years, you may be deriving some benefit from it without being aware of it. If, for example, you realize that you often complain about doing all of a particular area of work in the relationship, you may be feeding a sense of martyrdom. Martyrdom can provide a type of identity, that of the hard-done-by wife/husband/friend. Most people don't perceive that they are playing this game because it becomes so unconscious and ubiquitous. It can become a delicious role, providing countless opportunities to complain and to receive sympathy from others. It is, however, a role that puts the power in someone else's hands. Being a martyr is being a victim. By thinking about the questions I posed above, you may decide you want to make a change.

It can be frightening to change your way of behaving so that you are guided by your self-respect. Almost instantly you begin to see all the areas in your life in which you have put yourself aside for the sake of avoiding conflict. Though you may have justified your actions as self-sacrificing for the good of the relationship, that is a self-deception. A strong relationship is one that maintains the dignity, integrity, and self-respect of each person by maintaining a balance of giving and receiving on both sides. To take back your power, you must make the decision to become responsible for yourself and your own needs, and the needs of those in your care. By taking care of yourself, you maintain the emotional and physical energy to give; it also cultivates the self-respect that allows you to ask for what you need from your partner. Those who do not take care of themselves eventually become emotionally and often physically depleted and end up with little to give.

Make it clear to your partner what you need and want, once you evaluate what that is. Be open to your partner's responses. Of course, if you are both happy with how things are, that is fine. Enjoy! Respect is a two-way street. It is for the couple to negotiate the terms of *mutual* respect. If one member of a couple feels disrespected, there is not mutuality. The husband of one couple I saw in therapy consistently felt disrespected by his wife's lighthearted jokes about his weight. The wife kept saying, "It's a joke. Get over it." But the husband didn't laugh. He didn't find it funny. His wife was not listening to what he was saying, nor was she paying attention to how her husband experienced her "joke." If a joke isn't enjoyed by everyone involved, if a joke hurts someone, it isn't funny. On the flipside of that, if a person holds onto the unintended hurt of a joke and never forgives someone who is willing to acknowledge a mistake, that person is holding the other in emotional hostage. Why not accept a sincere apology? Human beings make mistakes. What is the purpose being served by holding onto a hurt? Genuine apologies and forgiveness are both part of a mutually respectful relationship.

What might be perfectly acceptable for one couple may not be for another. Each relationship is unique. However, if you are afraid of making your needs known to your partner, seriously consider what kind of relationship you have. Are you afraid to speak up because you have been threatened? Or is that threat something from your past that has no reality in the present? Is it just a bad time for your partner, or is it *always* a bad time, and consequently your needs are continually put on the backburner? In a good relationship, both parties are content and feel respected. If one party isn't, the relationship is one-sided. Though there is compromise in a relationship and there may often be times when you must put your own needs aside, those times are easier to weather in a relationship where mutual respect exists and flourishes.

I am not suggesting that we should consistently put our own needs, wants, and desires in front of everyone else's. That would lead to an extremely selfish world indeed. There must be a balance of interests, a balance of respect in ourselves and for others. I am really talking here about respecting ourselves and finding authentic generosity within to give to others.

The Power of Letting Go

IF YOU DECIDE that a relationship has to end because your partner or your friend doesn't treat you in the respectful way you wish to be treated, so be it; you can teach the next person in your life how it will have to be. It is only when you are able to let go, to allow things to take their own course, that you can establish what you will or will not tolerate. Sometimes it is only when the other person realizes that you are willing to walk away that he or she finds the motivation to consider his or her behavior and its impact. Or else you do move on.

With Harry, it was not until the day I was at the beach and he refused to listen to me that I finally discovered the power of leaving him behind. Once I decided to let go of controlling Harry and what might happen if he were left alone on the beach, Harry responded immediately to my turning my back on him. Harry had been refusing to listen. I had no other recourse. It is not something that can work often, and you must have a strong relationship for the dog to notice that you are not there, but when it works, it is powerful. For it to work, you must be willing to let go and accept the consequences of the act.

A dear friend of mine who is interested in finding a partner and starting a family began dating a man. In the past she has fallen in love with two men, both of whom were rich, powerful, and handsome. The relationships did not last, but not through her choice. After a few weeks of dating a new man, she experienced something that upset her. Previously she would not have jeopardized her relationship by bringing up something that bothered her; she would have stifled the feeling and carried on overtly happy and covertly hurt. This time she talked to the man about how she felt, knowing that doing so might potentially end their budding relationship. His lack of response to her concerns clearly indicated that he was not the kind of man she cared to continue with. She ended the relationship on her own, feeling empowered and clearer about what she wanted in a relationship with a life-partner.

In contrast, I have a client who is unhappy in her marriage. She feels that she has tried everything to convey to her partner the ways that they must change to create a better relationship. She is unwilling to let go, so she holds back some of what she could say that might make a difference, because that difference might be that he would decide he didn't want to save their relationship. To be ready to stand for what you want no matter what the consequences isn't ever easy, but it is always powerful.

Seeing Both Sides

I RECENTLY HAD A difficult conflict with a friend in which I felt disrespected. I thought that whatever I had done, I did not deserve the disrespect that he was showing me. In the past, I would have apologized for the situation and hoped to smooth over the conflict, but this time I was clear that I had to regain my self-respect, my dignity. I knew I could not control what he did or how he responded, but what I could do was set forth what I felt was wrong with the situation and how it affected me. I talked to him about the situation. Every time he attempted to minimize the effect his actions had, I respectfully brought him back to the facts of what had happened and what those effects were. But I also made a mistake. Because I had already decided how I thought he would react, I didn't really listen to what his response was.

The next day, I began to really think about our conversation and slowly I started to see his side of our argument. I had been so insistent on getting him to see my point that I had left very little room for him and his feelings. I am lucky that he cared enough about our friendship to allow me to dominate the argument with my side. We managed to work through the impasse with respect, and both of us came out with a deeper understanding of our friendship and ourselves. Never before in a conflict have I ever felt so fully heard, nor heard someone else so completely.

When your habitual way of handling a situation is to disrespect yourself, it can be difficult to find the right balance in your relationships. When you go overboard the other way, conflicts can easily become power struggles in which you feel you must confront and tenaciously hold your position to maintain your self-respect. That method risks losing valuable people in your life because you leave little or no room for someone else's perspective or feelings. As I look back on some of my conflicts, I begin to see myself as a pit bull rather than as the victim I had often felt myself to be.

Try to listen to the other side of the conflict without prejudice, without preconceived ideas about what the other may be feeling. You may find in many cases that both sides of a conflict have legitimacy. We perceive issues through our own particular lens but we have to acknowledge that others' perceptions can be valid too. When we step back to identify the particular lenses through which we view our life, we realize that we have the power to alter our perceptions and beliefs if we want to. Faulty perceptions can be changed, and that can help ourselves and our relationships.

When I was in my early twenties and very shy and insecure, I had a group of friends who seemed to be leaving me out of certain social activities. I waited and watched while they made arrangements with each other to do this or that. I became more and more guarded with them. I started feeling depressed and unworthy. Finally one day I got really angry and asked why they didn't like me anymore. They roared with laughter. They had been wondering why I didn't like them any more; when they talked about doing all kinds of great stuff I hadn't joined in or expressed any interest in what they were doing. They said I had seemed distant and unhappy with them. Still enraged, I told them they never invited me along anymore; they asked me since when did I need an invitation to be with them? That day changed the way I relate to friends forever after. Now, I no longer assume I know everything that is going on and I check out my perceptions because I know how often I have been mistaken. I also don't wait to be invited if I want to be involved.

Conflicts need an open mind, an open heart, and the ability to adequately distinguish your own and others' hidden agendas. Our tendency is to think it is always the other person who has the hidden agenda, but often we do, too. The agenda might be, "This time I will prove I have self-respect. This time I will win this argument because I lost the last one. This time I will not give in. This time I will not surrender." We need to develop our awareness of our deep pains, our hidden agendas, our self-deceptions, and to practice honesty with ourselves.

Because of Harry, I pay attention to how others behave towards me. I refrain from making excuses for people who treat me badly. To do so would only lead to lengthening a relationship that is doomed to fail and generates a sense of unworthiness in me. If I allow someone to be disrespectful to me without saying something about it, I am not respecting myself and not being courageous enough to be honest. Don't allow others to abuse you, and don't abuse others.

What did Harry actually teach me? In a nutshell, Harry taught me the importance of self-respect and courage in the face of fear, which naturally led to accomplishing things that I previously felt were impossible — communicating with an aggressive dog, writing this book, and dealing powerfully in a troubled relationship. It is in those moments when something very difficult, some challenge, is faced and overcome, that a whole person is created. That is how self-esteem comes to be.

My Father Taught Me

BILL RUSSELL, THE African-American basketball player and coach, told a story in an Arts and Entertainment *Biography* feature that encapsulated his stand on respect. Russell said, "I never allowed anyone to disrespect me. I learned it from my father." When Russell was a young basketball player, he traveled with his team. In a motel they were staying at, one of Russell's black teammates went to join his white teammates in the dining room. He was refused service and, as he left the room, he ran into Russell. He told Russell that the black team members would not be served. Russell said simply, "Then I am going home." The coach discovered what had happened and complained to the hotel general manager. To compensate for not allowing the black players in the dining room, the manager invited the black players from the team to his room for a private dinner. Bill Russell refused, saying, "I don't know the GM. I just want to have dinner." The four men left the hotel.

Bill Russell went on to become the first black coach in the NBA. In Russell's first press conference, he was asked by a reporter, "Will you be fair to the white players?" Bill Russell drew in a deep breath and responded, in his characteristic direct way, that respect is always what is important. He said he had respect for how a player plays.

No Excuse for Abuse

PEOPLE SOMETIMES find themselves in a relationship in which they are being abused. This should never be tolerated. Generally, if we allow one incident of abuse to occur, it gives permission for the possibility of more and greater abuses of ourselves or of others. "While unconditional love may be fine in theory, what if your partner treats you rudely and with disrespect? Allowing yourself to be hurt emotionally or physically is a perversion of empathy, which insists on respect as a foundation for every relationship," Arthur Ciaramicoli writes in *The Power of Empathy*. Abuse can be the physical, mental, or emotional torture of another. It disrespects the value of another.

Some abusers blame alcohol, some blame their partners for causing them to react so abusively, some blame their childhood, and others blame society for their actions. They place blame outside themselves as though their behavior was not in their control. Rather than blaming others for their responses, these people need to look inside themselves for the source of the problem.

Some victims often feel that if only they hadn't said "x," their partner wouldn't have been set off in a tirade of abuse. They are likely suffering from a deficiency of self-respect. They may have grown up in a household where an abusive parent blamed the children for not being quiet enough, bright enough, good enough. They have somehow become accustomed to taking the blame. These people need to begin to shed the belief that they are responsible for someone else's disrespectful or abusive behavior. If — in the rare occasion — they actively contribute to an abusive situation, they need to end the cycle, because it almost never gets better. Often an abuser finds a complementary victim who gives permission for the abuser to exercise his or her disrespect unchecked. If there is any danger in attempting to change an abusive relationship, the victim needs to seek an expert, a therapist, or a shelter.

Conflict and Peace

CONFLICT IS CENTRAL to our world. On a micro level, we are sometimes in internal conflict with ourselves. Often, we are in conflict with our families, friends, and extended relatives. Movies and novels revolve around conflict because it is what is interesting to us. Communities are often in conflict with the interests of the larger city, and so on.

The conflicts that erupt between people, between dogs, or between dogs and people are not much different than the ones afflicting nations. Darryl Reanney, in *Music of the Mind*, describes conflicts as being the fracturing of the one into many, with a driving desire to reunite. The Dalai Lama, in *The Book of Wisdom* and *The Power of Compassion*, talks about discovering the "other" in ourselves. The Dalai Lama believes that when we cease to dismiss others as being irrelevant to us but think of the complexity and interconnectedness of life and all living beings, we move towards a personal transformation that brings greater peace and compassion to the world. The Dalai Lama says in *Ancient Wisdom, Modern World*, "Because self and others can only really be understood in terms of relationship, we see that self-interest and other's interests are closely interrelated ... your interest is also my interest ... our interests are inextricably linked, we are compelled to accept ethics as the indispensable interface between my desire to be happy and yours."

Peacemaking, whether it takes place in nations engaged in conflict or in our own backyards, takes us one step closer to compassion, to understanding the thoughts and feelings and experiences of another, and to respect. It is when we come to understand another viewpoint and not impose our own as the "right" or "correct" one that peace has an opportunity to transcend the interests that fail to take into account the experience of another. We should "never confuse self-respect, our valid sense of participating in the world for the good of all with ego, our invalid sense of possessing the world for the good of one," says Darryl Reanney in his impassioned plea for us to forgo our selfish interests and look towards the greater context of the universe. Paradoxically, when we learn to accept the differences in each other, we actually come closer into union. Perhaps that is why so many people resist respecting differences in races, religion, ideas, and opinions: they fear what is different, and they fear themselves.

When Love Is Not Enough

ONE SEGMENT OF a beautifully inspired television documentary called "In the Company of Horses" illustrated profoundly the connection between love and respect. The horse's name was Biko and his owner was a paraplegic who loved her horse intensely. Her life dream was to ride her horse. But because of her paraplegia and the unrestraint of the horse, she had not been able to ride Biko. Her love for Biko was obvious, and Biko's love for her was just as powerful. The problem lay in the lack of boundaries created for Biko. In a way, Biko was a horse who loved her owner almost to death. During a demonstration, Biko knocked her owner out of wheelchair and almost walked on her. There was love, but no respect, no communication. I felt as though I were watching Harry and me. The trainer took Biko and the owner and taught them how to communicate and create respect by creating boundaries. Now Biko lies down for her owner to "climb aboard." For a horse, lying down is an even more vulnerable position than it is for a dog. The trust and respect that has to exist for Biko to lie down is astonishing. The depth of love that is now possible with the trust and respect that has been established will continue to grow.

When I read Elizabeth Marshall Thomas's book *The Social Lives of Dogs*, her deep love and respect for her dogs struck me. The dogs were allowed their expression of their individual personalities so long as they mastered the basic skills required for safety: come, sit, stay. I loved Thomas's appreciation of the true nature of dogs. Her stunning description of how one dog, Pearl, shrewdly trained her to wake up earlier and earlier was precisely my experience with the subtle training that Harry gave me and still to this day attempts. Thomas was satisfied to allow Pearl to determine the time she woke up. I, however, am not satisfied to allow Harry to train me into the behaviors that he desires. His desires seem far more self-serving than Pearl's. Harry uses his training to unravel my authority over him. Harry ekes out an inch and deftly takes a mile.

Harry's first attempts to train me were pure intimidation. He growled, I backed off. As I became more sophisticated, so did he. At one point I found Harry stopping suddenly during our walks. I thought he was getting hot and tired, so I politely stopped and allowed him to catch his breath. He would sometimes drop to the sidewalk for a minute or two. This confirmed my belief that Harry was getting hot. It was, after all, summer in the city. People would walk by and emit sympathetic sounds and ask how old Harry was. They were always surprised to hear Harry was barely two and a half years old. I was careful not to walk too far for too long if it was hot. I always took Harry out early, before the sun started beating down on the sidewalks, or after the sun began to slip behind the buildings. It was not until I walked with Suzanne, my first dog trainer, and she saw Harry stop and drop dramatically to the pavement that I learned I was being taken for a ride. She laughed hysterically at my explanation. Harry's acting talents were revealed to me that day.

Suzanne pointed out that Harry has amazing stamina for running. If a cat or a squirrel had trotted by, Harry would have leapt to his feet and run for hours. Harry was an actor pure and simple. He doesn't like walking on the lead, though he is really good at it. He likes to be free and running, not walking along a sidewalk where he can't sniff and mark at will. I was being slowly trained to allow Harry to stop whenever he felt like it. It is not the first time Harry has trained me, and he continues to get craftier and craftier with his wily ways. Charles Eisenmann, owner and educator of the original Littlest Hobo, writes in his brilliant book about dog training by the intellectual method, "A dog applies half his intelligence trying to obey you and learn what you ask of him, and the other half is devoted to finding ways to get around what you have said."

Strategies for Healing Disrespectful Relationships

STEP ONE: BECOME AWARE OF DISRESPECT

If you have lived your life allowing disrespect, you may not be adept at locating the sources as such instances occur. If you are at this stage, you need to develop your awareness so that you can get better and better at identifying the sources of disrespect in your life. Pay attention to the faint inner voice of intuition that says to you that something doesn't feel quite right. It might be as subtle as butterflies in your tummy. It may be the vague sense that there is something to say. Don't worry if you don't know exactly what it is; in time, as your awareness increases, you will become quite discerning. If friends or family have mentioned something to you, you may want to consider that they are seeing or sensing something that you are not allowing yourself to see. Most friends and family have your best interest at heart. It is only the rarest of occasion that a friend or family member wishes you unhappiness. Do you have just a vague sense that something is wrong or do you know that when so-and-so did such-and-such you felt this or that?

Learn to recognize your internal cues. I know when I feel disrespected because I feel numb, I loose the connection from my mind to my mouth, and I become silent. I have a vague sense that there is something I should be saying. Other people may feel angry, or guilty, unworthy, or filled with self-doubt — it is different for each person. It takes awareness to locate feelings of disrespect, and courage to address the issues, and trust to know that the other person will not attack you for your feelings.

Looking at complaints can be a path to learning how to discern respect issues. I have a client, I will call her Christine, who constantly complained that her husband no longer was affectionate with her, wouldn't look at her in the eyes, and took her for granted. By exploring these complaints she began to understand that she felt disrespected and that she was unhappy with the relationship the way it was.

It is at this stage that we also need to develop our ability to be honest with ourselves about our own hidden agendas. Otherwise we risk becoming hard-headed, as I did with my friend. It is no good proving a point when a relationship is ruined by it. When at all possible, we want to create a win-win situation. (There are times in life when a win-win strategy will not work and will in effect be a detriment to our self-respect, such as in instances involving court cases, persistent bullies, or abusive spouses.)

We have all experienced situations in our lives that just haven't been fair. It wasn't fair that after all the love and care I bestowed on Harry, he bit me. It wasn't fair that my mother got cancer and died. Apartheid wasn't fair. Segregation wasn't fair. The wrongful imprisonment of Ruben Hurricane Carter wasn't fair. (Ruben Hurricane Carter is the American boxer wrongly imprisoned for twenty-five years accused of a triple murder he didn't commit and was the subject of Bob Dylan's song "The Hurricane" and of the movie of the same name featuring Denzel Washington.) And it wasn't fair that my nephew got a smaller bowl of popcorn than his friend.

STEP TWO: ACCEPT REALITY

Dr. Phil McGraw, life strategist, friend, and consultant to Oprah Winfrey during her court case when she was sued by the Texas Beef Industry, gives a clear analysis in *Life Strategies* of what we must do to handle situations that are not fair. Dr. McGraw says, "Get real." He advises to get real fast and accept the reality of the situation rather than bemoaning the unfairness of it all. Create a strategy that accepts the reality of whatever you are facing. When my friends complain about a problem and want me to soothe their troubled souls, I often joke to them, "Deal with it! Get on with it! Get over it!" I am considered compassionate and empathic, but I like to be direct. It doesn't do anyone any good to shy away from problems, to sweep them under the carpet, or to treat them as unimportant. We can't forget about our problems or treat them as less important than other larger problems. We need to treat ourselves as important, as worthy, and as capable of dealing with our problems.

Once my client Christine began accepting the reality of her marriage, she moved into a new stage of dealing with disrespect. Christine asked her husband to enter into therapy with her to deal with their problems. She began to speak her truth about how disrespected and unloved she felt with him, and her honesty moved him to talk about how he was feeling. He had lost his love for her and felt that he wanted to divorce. The couple began to get real with each other, yet managed to maintain respect and dignity for their past love and the fact that they had a child together.

STEP THREE:
CREATE A STRATEGY FOR CHANGE

Once you have identified disrespect in your life, learning to deal effectively with it can be a challenge. Often when we feel disrespected we feel quite vulnerable and our reactions are more suited to attack or protection.

My clients, Christine and her husband, Paul, teetered on the edge of attacking each other and protecting themselves in an effort to avoid harsh truths. Both had felt years of being misunderstood and mistreated, and those feelings are powerful. Initially in the process, Christine felt quite vulnerable to Paul because she wanted to save her marriage and believed she still loved Paul. Slowly, as Christine came to respect herself, she realized that the marriage she really desired did not exist between her and Paul. Christine and Paul began to talk seriously about separation and divorce. Their strategy was to be open and honest with each other in therapy about how they were feeling. They would respect each other's feelings, and they would treat each other with civility, especially in front of their child. I also encouraged them to respect each other as wonderful parents. Both of them are great parents and care for their child deeply but had entered into a dangerous game of "I care more than you do."

Once Christine and Paul began to openly and honestly express their feelings, and Christine began to respect herself, something new entered into their relationship — mutual respect began to flourish. They are talking about the possibility of staying together and rekindling their love. It may or may not be possible, only time will tell. The critical element to success in this possibility is if Christine is capable of noticing when she experiences disrespect and building her self-respect.

It is unrealistic to expect that issues of respect will never arise in relationships. Respect is something that is negotiated in the relationship. That is why it is so important to learn how to recognize what you are feeling and to have the courage to speak up. Just because we feel that we are being disrespected doesn't necessarily mean it is so. Often simply asking what the intention was behind an action or statement will clarify whether it is an issue that needs to be negotiated.

STEP FOUR: STRATEGIES FOR HEALING

Dr. Harvey Freedman, my mentor, coined a term he called the five-minute-cure. It was unrealistic to believe that you could necessarily eradicate a lifetime habit, emotional process, or natural propensity, but it was realistic to learn how to notice our patterns within five minutes and learn not to become hostage to them. That was the five-minute-cure. First you learn how to recognize, to build awareness of, your patterns, then you learn what inhibits your call to action and how to summon the courage to take action.

I have a client, Allan, who loves to help other people. He always listens to his friends when they have problems. He has a demanding boss who he constantly tries to please. Allan doesn't feel worthy of any respect, so he keeps doing things for others, hoping that respect will be forthcoming when they realize how nice he is. Unfortunately for him, respect has not only not been forthcoming but was becoming less and less a possibility until his life began crashing down around him. Allan was trying so hard that he kept making mistakes, and the people in his life felt no compunction about adding to his misery. He believed that trying harder and harder to please people would eventually bring about a change in his life and theirs. He believed that he was bringing about harmony by not confronting the reality of each situation in his life.

This is not the harmony or wholeness that I am talking about, for Allan's relationships were not serving the whole but only one part — the part that was all for someone else and nothing for him. Allan is working towards the five-minute-cure. He now notices — about a day later — those instances in which he has forgotten himself in his own equation. A day later is a substantial step ahead of the months it used to take him to sort out where he had lost his sense of self-worth. Every situation is now an opportunity for Allan to decrease the time it takes him to become aware of when he has not been respecting himself by standing up for himself.

I had a conversation with a good friend, a very talented psychologist, who also has a grown-up son. Recently he came back from the West Coast and she allowed him and one of his friends to stay with her until they resettled. It was a reminder to her about how easy it is to lose oneself when around a loved one. Her boundaries had become blurry. Her son and his friend slowly gained ascendancy in her own house, until she finally put her foot down and instituted some rules. Of course, her son and his friend put up initial resistance, then were happy to oblige. After all, it was her home, the rules were fair, and her son and his friend had no problem accepting the limits she established.

The Disrespectful Friend

A FRIEND WHO IS constantly degrading you, either when you are alone or in front of others, is behaving disrespectfully. If, when you let your friend know how he or she is making you feel, your friend disregards your feelings, you may want to reevaluate whether you want that person in your life. If you look at the entire context of the relationship, you can begin to see whether the friendship is worth working on.

Perhaps your friend has driven you while your car was in the shop, helped you clean out your basement, made you dinners when you were tired, and brought you ginger ale when you were sick. Then she makes a passing comment about how your profession is one where there are little or no ethics. You will probably feel insulted by the comment. You tell her that her comment hurt you, or insulted you, and she says, "Get over it. Don't be so sensitive. I wasn't referring to you, just everyone else in your profession." You will probably still feel insulted and now you will likely feel unheard, but in the context of the friendship over time, this friend has shown great friendship. You may choose to end the friendship over the comment, but you may choose to disregard one comment within the context of a lot of other good. This is one of those not-so-clear-cut examples that we struggle with.

I have a friend who can trigger me by her off-hand comments that I interpret as her intimating I am stupid. For a while I felt completely controlled by my knee-jerk reactions, which caused me to snap back with either a defensive stance or more likely a sharp jab to the heart. Now I try to stop, gather my thoughts, and ask her why she would want to say something that hurts my feelings. The first time I managed this, she was taken aback by my response. She had gotten used to my gut responses, the usual outcome of which was me apologizing for being so caustic. Several hours later, I would still feel that something wasn't right, but I couldn't figure out how to put things back in balance — not until I slowed down my responses to the point where I registered the initial hurt to me and realized that it was my hurt that initiated my snappy and caustic responses.

This is a simple example of what can happen between friends. What happens between marital partners can become much more complex because they spend more intimate time together and learn subconsciously how to get in their digs. It becomes an escalating disaster of hurts upon hurts upon hurts. There may be a power imbalance in a marital couple at work as well. One partner may be physically stronger, or emotionally larger, or make more money, holding the other partner hostage. The partner held hostage often feels powerless to change the course of events and may come to perceive himself or herself as a victim. The dance becomes endless and can become quite dangerous.

Are you a victim or a victimizer? Or both? A person can be sometimes a victim and sometimes a victimizer. Be honest. Get professional help if you are unable to help yourself. There is nothing wrong with consulting a professional when your life feels as though it might be on a collision course.

Triggers

IDENTIFY YOUR TRIGGERS in life. If someone you love offends you by questioning your honesty and you are triggered into an angry response, begin the practice of becoming aware of that trigger. Then think about alternative ways you may want to react. Practice having no response, for example. Slow your responses down to the point where you can identify what set you off.

A Process for Managing Triggers
Using the Four Cornerstones

1. Be courageous: Identify the trigger and talk about it.
2. Be trusting: Trust yourself and others to be able to deal with the issue, but don't be blind to behavior that can harm you.
3. Be respectful: Don't blame others or yourself. Deal with the issue.
4. Be loving: Choose your reaction based on what will be the most satisfying to your relationship and to yourself.

Moving On

FOCUS OUTWARDS ONTO others and onto the world. There is not a whole lot you can do about your life when you are constantly blaming yourself or blaming others. Take responsibility for the effects you have in life. Chances are, if you are not able to see the harm you might be causing, you are also not seeing the good you are causing. Begin to live a life of integrity. It is not too late. If you have done terrible things in your life — and probably you have, as we all have, as I have — move along to right those wrongs, if possible. If someone has wronged you, you don't have to agree with what they have done, or condone their wrongdoing to move along yourself. Give up holding onto resentments that only hang like albatrosses around your neck and keep you from getting on with your life.

Animals are lucky. Harry never thinks back to the day he bit me. He isn't burdened by guilt, nor is he bound by resentment towards me for the lack of clarity and leadership in my training of him. He just moves on, each moment a new one. If you think that Harry is not capable of intelligent thought, remember this is a dog that has manipulated me. This is a dog that learned how to think about his actions and the consequences before reacting. He is quite capable of thinking, he has an excellent memory, yet he lives in the moment. Harry learns from the past, but he does not hold onto his emotional past.

In life there are disrespectful friends, mates, children, bosses, and coworkers. It is up to each individual to learn how to pay attention to what is going on in the relationship and to choose how he or she wants to deal with it. Don't get caught up in having to be right or proving you are right. Truth rarely lives in one place. Each person perceives his or her own truth of a situation.

Respecting Others

THE MARRIAGES THAT work are the marriages in which mutual respect exists and is in practice every moment of every day. Marriages work when each partner thinks about what is truly important to the other, cares about it, and does something about it. Often a marriage will appear to work for a while, and when it blows up, everyone thinks, "But they were so happy!" When the relationship was created at one person's expense, over time the lopsided relationship topples. A one-sided relationship can often be saved if the balance of respect can be redressed. Those partners who get everything must be willing to give up some of those goodies. Those partners who have been used to giving up themselves for the sake of peace need to learn a more direct and honest way of dealing with themselves and with their partners to create a balance.

Establishing Boundaries

LIMIT SETTING, OR establishing boundaries, is absolutely vital to establishing respect. We set limits for our children, our mates, our coworkers, our friends, and our dogs.

Dogs are very similar to children except — or maybe especially — the way they think is not always obvious to grown-ups. Many dogs bark to get back into the house when they are let outdoors in the morning to do their business. The owner thinks the dog has learned a form of doggy politeness, knocking on the door to say he is ready to come in. The dog thinks, "I bark, she jumps! Great!

I am really in control here." Or a dog owner picks up a leash and the dog begins to turn circles in anticipation of the walk. The owner thinks, "Oh, isn't that cute, Rover knows it's time for his walkies." Rover thinks, "Walkies! This is way cool, I have got them sooooo trained!" The dog is more interested in the walkies than in just being able to spend time with the owner. The dog sees the leash and does a little dance of anticipation because he knows the walk will always happen.

Adam Stone suggests you pick up your leash several times a day and never go anywhere with the dog. It teaches the dog not to expect and not to anticipate. The dog isn't happy just to be with the owner; the dog is always looking for what the owner will do for it. If this sounds harsh, it isn't meant to be. It is just meant to put into perspective how we cater to our dogs' whims and sometimes consequently create attitudes of entitlement. As Adam says, how many people do you see in the park in the early evening with their work clothes on? They usually say their dog couldn't wait to get out to walk, so they had to go for the walk immediately. We must teach our dogs some patience. They can wait while we change our clothes to be more comfortable during a walk. It becomes a case of the pet behavior training the owner, rather than the other way around. I have joked that my mantra is, "I am not Harry's pet. I am not Harry's pet."

Charles Eisenmann talks about humans bringing the dog into the human's world and not the other way around. It makes sense to me. I had been so interested in communicating with Harry that I worked towards understanding him, rather than teaching Harry to understand what I wanted from him. Once I started raising Harry's level of thinking, the world became a different place for both of us and respect naturally grew out of that. I stopped making Harry the center of my interest and instead made Harry interested in me.

How Did It Get Like This?

A WOMAN CAME TO me for therapy in a terrible state. She was addicted to drugs and alcohol and was clearly unhappy with the way her life was going. First she got detoxified, then she started to look at what in her life led her to her choices and what kind of life she dreamed of creating for herself. She asked me why people might treat themselves with such lack of respect, as she had to herself. This beautiful, young woman put herself in abusive relationships, was sexually active with numerous partners and strangers without protection, and wished herself dead. The story she grew up with was that her mother hadn't gotten along with her since the day she was born, unlike the other four children in her family, who were apparently fine. This young woman was deemed bad from the moment of conception. "Your father was off the day you were conceived," her mother would joke, not noticing the pain her joke caused. Though the woman was from a wealthy family, she lived a life similar to many unfortunate children from underprivileged families, or those in which there is alcohol abuse: a succession of group homes, early sexual abuse, foster families, and eventual prostitution.

Her plaintive question of why she might be treating herself this way and the story of how she grew up reminded me of how sometimes parents and babies are badly paired. The parent either doesn't have the knowledge, the tools, the personality, or the inclination to "be" a different way to meet the early needs of the infant. Some babies need a mother who is stimulating, energetic, and active, whereas others need a mother who is calm, secure, and confident. Some colicky babies cry a lot, and some mothers aren't able to handle that. Perhaps they feel the child is rejecting them, or they aren't good enough mothers. Or perhaps they blame the babies for being bad for crying, or for never being satisfied with anything they as mothers do. The early relationship with mother and baby can have profound effects on how both relate as the child grows. My client was constantly seen as a bad baby, a bad child, so by the time she was a teenager, she lived into the role that had been defined for her. She became the bad teenager, rejecting authority, running away, acting out sexually, and living dangerously.

This client is now in the process of deciding what kind of life she wants to live. How she wants to be in life and how she is going to live that. She possesses a great deal of kindness and integrity, and good people have rallied to support her. She calls them angels, but I believe that the good people she is attracting are more a reflection of who *she* is; a woman with a good heart and an open soul but who has been very mixed up about who she is or could be. This woman has suffered terribly from low self-esteem established at a young age in childhood through the mis-matched mother-infant bond. She had never experienced love and so could not love and respect herself. All her unconscious acting-out behaviors underscored her self-hatred. She needed to be loved so she could learn to love herself, thereby gaining self-respect so that she would treat herself as someone who mattered and begin to demand that others respect her as well.

The personal journeys of our early life chart the course our later actions are likely to take. We all have different experiences that shape us. Becoming aware of our patterns helps us to become free from our habitual responses so that we may choose our responses more consciously.

Transcending the Cross-Species Divide

HARRY IS A STREET dog and his doggy instincts are sharp. He is excellent at navigating the dog world, particularly when he is off leash. He knows which dogs not to bother, knows which ones are safe to sharpen his fighting skills with, and knows which ones he can dominate. He knows how to find food, evade the animal control, and hide in cozy nooks in the winter. I've read about dogs in Italy and France, where dogs are allowed in many places they are not allowed in North America. These dogs manage themselves with dignity in restaurants and hotel lobbies. I hope that Harry will be able to navigate the people world that he lives in that well.

I want him to be able to think for himself, to manage himself, to make good decisions, much as we want our children to learn how to manage themselves and make good decisions. Harry wants to communicate. He tries to communicate. He wants respect but has to earn it, as we all must.

LESSONS IN RESPECT

- Speak up for yourself and your needs.
- Try to see the problem clearly without blaming yourself or others.
- Slow down and think before you react.
- Develop awareness of patterns in your life and think about what they may be telling you.
- Establish boundaries.
- Find your center so that you may deal with others from a self-respecting stance.
- Be prepared to sometimes let go and accept the consequences.
- Stay open to other points of view.
- Be aware of your own hidden agendas.
- Don't make excuses for people who treat you badly.

STRATEGIES IN RESPECT

- Become aware of disrespect from others.
- Accept the reality of the situation.
- Make a plan to deal with the situation that is respectful to yourself and to others.
- Recognize that it takes time to make changes.
- When you don't succeed, recognize that you will always have another chance.

Harry on Love:
More Than Give and Take

The time to judge friendship, love, faithfulness
or adoration is not when the going is smooth, but
when desires are curbed and adversity strikes.

— CHARLES EISENMANN
on the education of London,
the original Littlest Hobo.

HOW MANY ZILLIONS OF hours have I spent with clients
talking about love, or with friends discussing love, analyz-
ing love, dissecting love, questioning love, beginning love, ending love, hoping for love, vowing never to love again, falling in
love, resisting love, surrendering to love, denying love, and pre-
tending its importance is less than it is. I am not sure what this
says about me, but undeniably I have learned more about love
from my guru dog, Harry, than from any other experience. I
have loved intensely in my life. I have been hurt by love, and I
regretfully have caused hurt in love.

Why do I say that Harry, a mere canine, taught me what love
was about? When you love a human partner and things begin to

go badly, the tendency is either to blame yourself, or to blame the other, or to alternate between these two states. It is really difficult to blame a dog for problems in the relationship that arise, or, if the dog *is* the problem, to expect the dog to know how to fix things. You have to take the full responsibility for changing the direction that the relationship is going. You have to be the one to understand the dog's needs at the deepest level.

What has the guru taught me about love? He taught me patience. He taught me forgiveness. He taught me about the holes in my soul through which love could seep away one drop at a time. He taught me that I could no longer hide, for he would reveal me to myself. He taught me that it is in the darkest moments of a crisis that love is challenged. He taught me that I could no longer give without taking, take without giving. The Dalai Lama, the embodiment of love, talks of the practice of tong-len, of giving and taking as the practices of loving kindness and compassion.

The Dalai Lama writes in *The Book of Wisdom,* "For someone to develop genuine compassion towards others, first he or she must have a basis upon which to cultivate compassion, and that basis is the ability to connect with one's own feelings and to care for one's own welfare. If one is not capable of doing that, how can one reach out to others and feel concern for them? Caring for others requires caring for oneself."

This is just a small excerpt in a discussion about the Buddhist practice of tong-len that resonated with me. The Dalai Lama makes a distinction among four kinds of human behavior: valuing our own precious core so excessively that we disregard the well-being of another; self-hating that leads us to take on the miseries of others in a masochistic way; being indifferent to others; and endeavoring to truly consider the well-being of others. The Dalai Lama extends his compassion to all the sentient beings of this world and particularly to those we deem less than ourselves. The lessons that I learned from Harry and the love that developed from those lessons link to the Buddhist philosophy the Dalai Lama speaks of.

Love eludes definition for me, but I feel I must try to say something about what I think it is. Love is compassion. Love is the way we express the deep bonds we create with others in our life. When we live our lives with love, we treat others with respect and compassion. There are many different kinds of love: intimate love, romantic love, the love between parents and children, teachers and students, between siblings, friends, and humans and animals. There is the love of life, of nature, and of spirituality; there is the feeling of living life with love, passion, and awe for all things; there is acting with love whenever we do something with a loving intention. Each loving relationship is different, yet we can always recognize when love exists. We seem to be wired for love.

The courage to face our issues within ourselves and with other people, to trust that we can learn new ways to deal with them, and to respect ourselves and those with whom we deal prepares us to be open to love. We can learn to be compassionate and loving to ourselves and to accept the loving relationships we find in our lives. By finding my courage to try to build a new relationship with Harry, learning new skills I could rely on and trusting myself to use them well, and respecting Harry and myself, I was able to build the loving relationship I wanted to have with my dog. The interplay between the cornerstones to healing of courage, trust, and respect provides a deep and rich environment where love can then mature.

Loving Teachers

WHEN I MET ADAM STONE, I could not miss the deep love that he has for dogs. It is the most pure unconditional love that I have ever seen expressed. He does not, however, romanticize dogs. He never underestimates their capabilities for good or bad behavior, or their propensity towards opportunism. The wayward dogs that have found their path to Adam he sees clearly for the atrocities they have committed. He does not tolerate their bad behavior; but the love always comes through. He will chastise a transgressing dog, kiss his nose, then unceremoniously pop him into a kennel until the dog shows he is worthy of attention.

Adam has spent the past few years living on his farm with hundreds of aggressive dogs at a time. He told me that the experience he gained from the sheer volume of dogs was invaluable for understanding what makes dogs do the things they do. Adam is a keen observer of animal and human behavior. I have learned more than I ever thought possible about the interaction and relationships between owners and their dogs. The more I learn, the deeper my respect grows for Adam's knowledge and the canines he loves. His experience living with so many aggressive dogs has undoubtedly garnered him the position of the foremost expert on canine aggression and dog behavior.

What is unique about Adam? Well, there are many things, but one that stands out is his ability to observe a dog's behavior without prejudging the situation or anticipating what the problem is. He can then put together the elements that were there or not there during the dog's development and understand what that animal needs. Adam's basic philosophy for retraining aggressive dogs is deceptively simple. Don't add anything to the dog's training, just take away until the dog returns to a natural state and is open to learning and ready to begin building a loving bond.

When we share our life with dogs there is no doubt that it is an intimate experience, punctuated with times of peace, times of frustrations, times of great love, arguments, and learning about each other. But living with an aggressive dog places much greater demands on the owner than living with a docile dog does. We are forced to learn the complexities of the canine personality, our own personality, and how the two interact. We must understand the dog on his terms first and then invite him into a relationship of companionship that continues to develop and deepen with a shared language of respect, trust, and love. It becomes a relationship of deep love once the context for love has been set through the interplay of the cornerstones.

One day I walked with one of the local dog owners who owns a very well-behaved dog. He told me that he had thought he knew about dog handling and understood dogs until he dog-sat for a friend. The dog was a problem and he could not do a thing with it. He said he realized then it wasn't his knowledge that delivered him his wonderful, loving dog — his dog was just naturally wonderful. Lucky him!

All beings have different temperaments and require different treatment. Ask any mother who has more than one child to raise, or the dingo bitch I referred to earlier who treated her more rambunctious puppies differently from the others. It is an extraordinary act of love to take the time to learn how to treat individuals individually. Placid babies and pups often require more stimulation and encouragement from the mother, whereas boisterous babies and pups usually require stronger boundaries and a calmer approach.

I have noticed this loving attention to students from my ba gua chang teachers, Alex and James. Both are gifted in their study of the individual, of his or her strengths and weaknesses and current level of practice. They design their instruction to suit that person's needs. For example, I am a little dancey and flowing in my movements, so they instruct me to have more powerful intention with a quicker, more definite action. It counterbalances my graceful, dance-like qualities by building more powerful intention. My fellow student, Cesar, is harder in his practice, so his instruction is to become softer, using more fluid sweeping motions.

Love Doesn't Always Come Easy

YEARS AGO, MY work focused on delinquent teenagers. Working with these young people was extremely rewarding, as they did not let you into their lives instantly just because you said you were there to help them. In fact, that was often the reason for keeping you out. Some of these kids had had so much "help" from professionals that they were suspicious of anyone who offered it. They didn't let you in until they had decided that you deserved it, but once that happened, it was an extraordinarily experience. There was something simple, straightforward, and natural about that. Many of these kids had not had good experiences with their parents, and their experiences with other authority figures also had been less than stellar. They didn't love easily, they didn't love until it was earned, but when they did love, they loved with deep and abiding loyalty. These street kids had learned to take care of themselves in the most difficult of circumstances. They were streetwise beyond their years.

Harry reminds me of those streetwise teenagers. There are times when Harry is just in a mood. He doesn't want to be bothered. He doesn't want to think. He doesn't want to interact. I have to respect that. (Of course, if I don't respect that, he will bite me.) He is adept at taking care of himself and resents my intrusion into affairs he feels quite confident in handling himself. Also like those teenagers, he missed some foundation work of trust and of submitting himself willingly into the care of another when he was young. Harry's behavior early in our relationship indicated he had no experience with connecting to a human. He was uninterested in them. He had no intention of listening to one. So Harry and I had our work cut out for us. It is easier to lay the foundation before the building has been erected, or the baby has grown into a teenager, or the puppy into a dog, but it isn't impossible to go back and pick up lost stitches — to mix metaphors. It has been extremely rewarding to work so intensely with Harry, to help him get back to a natural open state. It is a tenuous balance for me to be strong enough to be a good leader to someone (well, some dog) who thinks he doesn't need anyone and also to be loving and gentle enough to gain his trust. The feelings cannot be faked. They are either genuine or they are not. Street dogs and street kids can tell or smell the difference.

The Mask

DURING MY PSYCHOTHERAPY training years, I was fortunate to find a mentor who was particularly sensitive to how people put forward niceness to conceal their unsavory intentions to themselves or towards others. When people are hiding themselves and their true feelings and intentions, they are creating an environment that is not conducive to allowing love to flourish. Here again it is time to become brutally honest with yourself. Sometimes it takes some training to understand what it is you might be trying to conceal. If you constantly talk about love and lovingness but have continued conflict in your life, you need to look at what you are trying to hide. Is there an unresolved anger eating away at you that you are trying to cover up with the love you wish to have in your life but don't? Love is a quite genuine feeling that is experienced deep in the gut and emanates outwards. As Dr. Phil McGraw might say, "Get real." If you have some unresolved anger, acknowledge it, let it go (reread the section on forgiveness in the chapter on respect). Don't try to hide behind a Band-Aid with "Love" written on it. That is superficial and does not heal the inner wounds. Love needs an open heart to penetrate and to bring its joys to fruition.

Some clients in my practice who complain bitterly about never receiving love in their lives from their mates, their parents, their siblings, or their friends are people who hide behind a veneer of niceness. These people need to uncover their hostilities, resentments, and bitterness. They need to heal their wounds by using the cornerstones of courage to honestly face themselves, of trust towards others to learn about themselves, and of respect towards others to discover that love begins to flow when they are released from their own bitter prison.

One of the main ideas in this book that I hammer away at is the importance of self-examination to "unconceal" your deceptions, the deceptions to others and to yourself. It is a difficult process but one that can truly transform your life and the life of others. The truer you are to yourself, the deeper your ability to love and be loved. M. Scott Peck writes the most compelling book about "the hope for healing human evil," in *People of the Lie*. His contention is that evil resides in everyday life when people hide behind a façade of loving-kindness, of niceness, and of respectability. Peck says, "Evil originates not in the absence of guilt but in the effort to escape it ... We see the smile that hides the hatred, the smooth and oily manner that masks the fury, the velvet glove that covers the fist." Evil people are dedicated to their own appearances of righteousness as though the appearance of righteousness is what matters. Peck believes that "some of us are very good and some of us very evil, and most of us are somewhere in between," struggling to maintain our integrity.

The practice of life requires that we constantly flex our muscles to more often make the "better" choice, the more "courageous" choice. Through each good choice we make, we become better, stronger, more whole, which allows us the freedom to love. That is why it is so important to practice first in small ways. If you feel tempted to tell a "little" lie because it is easier, don't. Face the music and tell it like it is. You will be taking one step towards a more courageous you, towards greater integrity. We all struggle with falling away from integrity, and our battle should be in how we regain it. Usually it is in confronting some reality that we have tried to hide from. Erich Fromm, psychoanalyst and social philosopher, says, "The longer we continue to make the wrong decisions, the more our heart hardens; the more often we make the right decision, the more our heart softens — or better perhaps, comes alive." By staying honest we allow the possibility of love to enter our lives in more meaningful ways.

In *Essential Sufism*, James Fadiman and Robert Frager write, "You cannot see the back of your own head, no matter how intently you stare into a mirror or how quickly you turn around. Even the most clear-sighted have blind spots. These places to which we ourselves are blind are often astonishingly visible to others. The sword of self-knowledge, the ability to see oneself clearly, spans the abyss of ignorance." I believe awareness is an essential ingredient for deepening love and intimacy, to become aware of our thoughts, our emotions, our intentions, and ourselves.

A Fast-track to "Love"

AT A PARTY CELEBRATING the first television airing of my friend Deborah Day's directorial debut, I was introduced to a dog trainer. We chatted and I relayed my experience with Harry. She told me about clicker training. "Why waste time?" she asked, "The clicker gives immediate results." The trainer was emphatic about the virtues of clicker training. To me it is an example of our desire for immediate results, quick-cures, and instant love without doing the work that builds a deep and lasting bond. The work is hard, of course, but extremely rewarding.

Clicker training was originally created to train dolphins. First, the trainer "powers" up the clicker. This is achieved through feeding the dolphin copious amounts of fish each time the clicker sounds. Obviously the clicker clicks! Once the dolphin connects the sound of the click to receiving a fish, the powering up is complete and the training begins. When the dolphin leaps out of the water, the clicker clicks and the dolphin gets a fish. Eventually the giving of the fish is removed and the dolphin performs to the sound of the click. Clicker training soon found its way into myriad methods of dog training.

Food-training dogs became extremely popular in recent decades. Like clicker training, food lures promise immediate results. You call your dog to come and hold a treat in your hand. The dog comes, eats the treat ... then runs away again. You hold a treat high in your hand and tell the dog to sit, and your dog, mesmerized by the yummy treat, sits up straight, waiting for you to deliver the goods. Is this love or greed in action?

When I first adopted Harry, he didn't care if I had a treat when I called him to come to me. He would much rather run free and play with the dogs than take the time to come grab a treat. On the odd occasion when he did come, he would take the biscuit and run. I would be reduced to helplessly racing after him, begging him to come to me while he dodged and deked like a multimillion-dollar football halfback. I swear he laughed at me during those times. I was not alone in the park. I witnessed more people than not vainly attempting to bribe their dogs into submission. We can mistakenly believe we have trained our dogs, when all we have done is condition them. We can believe they love us when no real bond exists. Feeding a treat to a dog to gain his love is tantamount to feeding bread to the birds to gain their affection. They may hang around, they may recognize you as the food person, but it will not be the reason they connect to you spiritually and lovingly.

Basis for Loving Bonds

CAN YOU IMAGINE bribing your child with a cookie to come home to you? Or promising your husband a biscuit if he will come to bed with you? Would you feel loved or used? What would happen if your child was promised a bigger cookie by a stranger? Or your husband promised gourmet meals by a gorgeous seductress? Would your child chose your little cookie or the double-chocolate cookie of the stranger? Your husband, a biscuit or a gourmet meal? Would you be confident that, when confronted with the choice, your loved ones would make decisions based on the "right" reasons — their deep love for you — and would you be confident that once they have made the choice, that choice was made with free will, and not out of fear, or obligation, or something else that may indicate a rift in the bonds you had hoped you had created.

You had better be confident of their choice or something is wrong in the way your bonds of love have been created. Love is more than what you do for someone else. It is more than having the best cookies to give, or the best dinners to serve, or the best treats for your dog. Love is built on the cornerstones of healing that we have talked about in this book. You might enjoy the generosity of someone and that may be a factor in why you are attracted to that person, but that isn't love.

My client, Christine, whom I mentioned in the previous chapter, wanted the love of her husband so much so that she resorted to similar tactics as the pet owners who try to bribe their dogs with treats. Christine put enormous effort into her looks to attract her husband, who had stopped looking at her. She thought she had done everything she could to earn his love, but his love needed to be freely given. It wasn't until Christine stopped trying to win his love by looking beautiful, keeping an immaculate house, and being a perfect mother to their daughter and started to look at the deeper issues of courage, trust, and respect that Christine began to find her self-respect and love slowly reentered their marriage.

I have several friends, each who have been married for many years, whose love is natural and forthcoming towards their partners. It is not as though there haven't been difficulties to navigate — there have been — but the difficulties were possible to navigate with courage because the commitment to love was there with a strong foundation of trust and respect. That is how the cornerstones to healing interact to give a solid base to relationships. When the basis is solid, the need to control outcomes and other people diminishes and eventually vanishes, because there is always a way to be open about your feelings. It is when couples stop being courageous about their feelings, or they fear disrespect and so stop the flow of openness that love becomes impaired and problems become insurmountable.

If you find yourself bending out of shape to meet what you think the needs of your partner are, you are headed for some unhappy times. Most of us, both men and women, do this to a certain extent, and it is never fulfilling for anyone, least of all to the person you are trying so hard to please. Eventually the pressure of trying to be something that you are not catches up to you. It seems when the love is right, there isn't anything you can do that is wrong. And when the love is wrong, there isn't anything you can do that is right. Be yourself.

Loving Connections

YOU KNOW YOU HAVE a bond with your dog when he would rather be with you no matter what you are doing. You know you have a solid bond with your dog when he focuses on you even in the face of distractions. When he looks deeply into your eyes even when a squirrel runs past. When he is confident enough in your shared intimacy that he can fall asleep by your side or get up and explore his world without you on his tail. Dogs who are not bonded move around their owners anxiously like an overexcited child looking to be entertained. Bonded dogs and their owners appear relaxed and confident. They are respectful of each other.

Connecting with a dog is a profoundly gratifying experience. Dogs are capable of loving so deeply and completely. They become such loyal trusted and trustworthy companions when we allow the love to develop naturally into a genuine bond. There are countless stories of the courageous acts dogs have committed in the service of their owners. In Santa Barbara, where I used to live, there is a beautiful statue of a dog. It honors a family pet that lost his life while saving the family from a house fire.

When I am in the park now, I am totally confident that Harry will come to me — most of the time. Not because I have a treat — I don't — but because he loves me, and he wants to be with me. Through the long process of building trust, respect, and love, Harry is bonded to me. I do not have to bribe Harry; I am his human, not his treat machine, and he loves me. I do not have to prove myself to Harry; we have achieved trust, and he knows I won't hurt him. I do not have to insist Harry obey me, because I do insist that he respect me. Even if Harry doesn't want to come to me, he does because I have asked it of him. You don't see mother dogs bribing their pups with treats to come to them. If her pups don't come, she grabs them by the scruff of their necks and carries them to where she wants them. They learn that she means business and they learn to comply. That isn't to say that there aren't times when Harry or any other extremely well-behaved dog might not stretch the limits when asked to come, but it is rare, and with the passage of time becomes even rarer.

Freedom and Security

IN HUMAN RELATIONSHIPS, people become overanxious for many reasons about their bonds or lack of bonds. It is important to stay in touch with how you feel in a relationship so that you can exercise your lessons in courage to express openly to your friend or partner how you are feeling. In that way, you can check your perceptions with reality — assuming your friend or partner is aware enough of themselves to be honest. If you are in an intimate relationship and you feel insecure about your shared bond, one of several issues may be in operation. You have intuited a breach in the bond and you need to ask if there is a change or if you are harboring an insecurity that exists only in your mind, and so need to ask your partner for a reality check. If your partner is a decent and sensitive person, he or she won't mind providing you with some comfort about your insecurity (unless his or her comfort constantly enters into a bottomless pit of need for security). Or your partner may not be providing you with a sense of security because he or she is unable or unwilling to. These are all issues that, with a little courage to express them, some trust that you will not be condemned for bringing them up, and mutual respect in discussing issues, will bring about profound changes in the foundations of your loving bond.

So often in intimate relationships — particularly in the beginning and then later when complexities or problems develop — people are fearful of allowing their feelings to be known. Past experiences and beliefs play an important role in what we fear and how we deal with problems. Men may be fearful of appearing needy, dependent, or insecure, as they often believe they should be powerful, independent, and self-sufficient. But feeling secure in an intimate relationship is vitally important for creating and maintaining trust and respect and ultimately the sense of freedom. Some women may be fearful of appearing needy, dependent, or insecure, as they believe that might frighten their partner and make him go away. But courageous communication about love is the only path to achieving a mutually respectful relationship built on trust. By addressing issues using the four elements, our intimate relationships can be strengthened, building strong loving bonds.

When in relationships, we often confuse attachment with commitment; recognizing the distinction between the two can help deepen the relationship. Attachment occurs when we have a preconceived belief of how things should be or what outcome must be achieved. This not only is limiting the possibilities of the relationship but, in many instances, it serves to imprison the relationship in a particular form. Commitment, on the other hand, occurs when we are committed to the relationship, or any process, without being wedded to a specific form or outcome. We remain open to possibilities within the relationship, whatever the outcome. So, for instance, if we are attached to the idea that a relationship between two people must have the form of living together and vacationing together, the relationship misses the possibility of evolving in other ways. One of the partners may wish to go on vacation with a friend instead of his or her partner, but that idea cannot even be entertained because it falls outside the realm of the couple's attachment.

An example of how this played out for Harry and me was my teaching Harry how to hold an object (a pen) in his mouth and walk with it. When I was attached to Harry holding the pen for me, Harry gave me nothing but attitude. I became frustrated and angry because Harry wasn't complying with what I wanted him to do. When I finally gave up being attached to the outcome — that Harry would hold the pen without giving me attitude — I could work on teaching Harry to hold the pen as a process. Harry's resistance no longer mattered; we were working on a process. I lost my frustration, and Harry experienced my commitment to teaching him to hold a pen, but he no longer experienced my frustration, so he held the pen. The distinction made a difference in the way I approach everything; with commitment and persistence, but without attachment to how I believed things should be.

As in my ba gua practice, I am committed to the practice but I am not attached to any particular notion of how the practice should proceed or what it will deliver me. Every day I experience what it brings. I do my practice as best I can with the best intention to continually improve. Attachments become prisons of the mind in that we are no longer open to possibilities; commitment is what gives us the freedom required to dedicate ourselves to pushing through resistance, bouts of boredom, defeats, and disappointments.

The following story epitomizes a relationship in which the couple is committed but not attached. I have a friend, Alicia, who grew up feeling unloved by her family. A tragic car accident in her early twenties changed her life forever. Alicia courageously accepted responsibility for her role in the car accident, gave up drugs and alcohol, and allowed love to enter her life through the care from her sisters, brothers, aunts, and uncles during her rehabilitation. Through this love, Alicia gained trust in herself and others. She entered therapy and developed self-respect through the honest confrontation with her past.

A decade and a half later, Alicia is happily living with a man, Alan, who not only loves and treasures her but accepts her fully with all of her insecurities, passions, and idiosyncrasies. Alicia learned her lessons well. She respects herself enough to know that her feelings are valid and important. She has enough courage to say to her partner what at one time she thought could not be said to someone whose love she desired. Alicia made it clear to Alan that she can become insanely jealous because of the competitiveness she felt early in her life with her four sisters and so she needs to feel that she is special to him. At the same time, Alicia and Alan agreed that the moment they felt that their love was lost or that someone else might be catching their attention, they would end the relationship before either one of them felt disrespected, trapped, or obligated.

They have been together for a little over ten years now and both partners are quite open and free in expressing their absolute respect, trust, and love for each other. Both Alicia and Alan feel they have security (they provide each other the security they each need) and freedom (neither wants the other to feel obligated to stay in the relationship if it is no longer desired).

The Language of Love

GARY ZUKAV SAYS about love in his book *The Seat of the Soul,* "If you cannot love yourself, you cannot love others ... If you cannot love yourself, loving others becomes a very painful endeavor with only occasional moments of comfort ... Love is contaminated because it is filled with sorrow for themselves."

Zukav is talking about the need to love ourselves in order to adequately love others. To love ourselves, we must at some point of our lives experience being loved. There are some people who unconsciously push love away when love is what they most desire. We need to become aware of what we do with our love, of how we behave when we are in love or are in need of love.

A client of mine, Rhonda, grew up in a profound state of need, having never experienced the love of her parents. She went from friend to friend, man to man, desperately seeking love and acceptance. Whatever love or acceptance was given dropped into a bottomless well of need. Her relationships with friends and with partners rarely lasted more than a few weeks. She would wear them out with her extreme dependency. In therapy, Rhonda discovered the courage to allow herself to experience love, first from her therapist, then from her sister, her brother, and a friend. Now, many years later, she is married with children.

Another client, Pat, was married to a wonderful man, but she had never truly accepted his love. She remained feeling unfulfilled, unloved, and unlovable, and attempted to rectify the problem by having countless affairs. In time, through therapy, she realized how she had blocked the love her husband had for her. She stopped having affairs and began loving and being loved by her husband and children. They developed beautifully over the years and they acquired deep intimacy in their marriage.

Dogs in the World of Humans

WHEN WE ARE TEACHING dogs how to behave in the world of humans, their capacity for trust, love, compassion, and devotion must be released first through the language of dogs. Some dogs develop problems, for whatever reasons. It is not always an abusive or an indulgent owner who ends up with a problem dog. Dogs are complex beings, and people often require expert help in understanding what they need to become the loving, compassionate friends they are capable of being.

I have not read anywhere or met anyone who seems to understand the language of dogs more than Adam Stone. He explains that everything the dog understands is first seen in terms of its own reference, that is, leadership and pack rules. That is why obedience commands do nothing or very little for handling aggressive dogs. Adam demonstrated this with an aggressive Neopolitan mastiff. When he commanded the dog to sit, the dog sat. He then began walking with the dog, which did not want to be pulled away from his owners and began growling, snarling, and lunging. Adam ordered the dog to sit, but the dog continued to growl, snarl, and snap viciously. The perfectly obedience-trained dog forgot everything it had learned when challenged in a fundamental way and would have surely torn the arm off someone if given the opportunity. The dog stayed with Adam for several months, undergoing a similar retraining experience as Harry's.

Dogs do not ask each other to sit, stay, lie down, or heel. These commands are man-made and have little relevance in the dog world. However, dogs do ask each other to respect their space, to settle down, to not act like a jerk, to keep with the pack, to run with the pack, to be quiet, to not run wild, to not run away, and other packlike codes of behavior. Adam takes problem pets and puts them into a neutral or natural state; the owners can then create a lasting, loving bond with them. Our job, then, is to take these domesticated pack animals and transform them into trustworthy house pets.

When Fear Turns to Love

I WANTED TO GET TO the bottom of Harry's aggression. After many months of working with Harry to develop trust and respect, I felt that there was still a bite waiting to happen given the right circumstances. I knew we had been developing a

bond and that we had become trusted companions, but I just felt
there was something deeper that I had yet to penetrate. To be perfectly frank, it still terrified me. Down deep, I could not deny that
there was something that Harry retained completely for himself
that I had yet to understand.

For the previous months I had managed to create the situations that allowed me to avoid the possibility of getting bitten, but
then one day, the unspeakable happened. A situation I could not
avoid. Harry was digging in my friend's garden to bury a bone.
He was intense. He was in his altered state. I recognized that it
would be dangerous to intervene, but my friend wanted him out
of her garden so I had to act. He wouldn't listen to my command,
so I grabbed his collar to pull him away and he bit me.
Immediately, Harry became sad and apologetic. I recognized that
he had not wanted to bite me but something I could not completely understand had driven him to bite. I did not ever want this
behavior to happen again.

I knew I had to deal with my fear. I thought that if I recreated a
scenario with Adam beside me, when Harry went into his altered
state, Adam might be able to decipher Harry's behavior. So one
morning we left Harry for about fifteen minutes alone outside
with a bone. Harry trotted from place to place with his bone with
increasing fervor. Once he settled on a spot at the back of the
house, Adam and I went to him. Harry was pushing the dirt over
his bone with his nose. Harry looked up and I recognized his
darkened look. He was thoroughly in his altered state. We had
engineered this scary state and now I was actually about to get
close to him. Adam crouched down and called to Harry to "drop."
Harry wheeled around, looking terrified and cornered. He snapped
at Adam. Adam pushed Harry's haunches and he wheeled around
snapping. Harry turned back and gently nosed the dirt back over
the bone. Adam, watching, asked, "Is that the way Harry always
buries his bone?"

"Yes. He always uses his nose."

"Your dog isn't burying his bones. You have a neutered, male dog who is nesting!"

We watched Harry enact the ritual exactly as I had watched him do many times before. Harry delicately pawed some earth away, placed the bone down, and gently nosed the dirt over the bone. He would stick his nose into the mound and blow air, then begin his ritual again. Adam got close to Harry and showed me what he wanted me to do.

"Get up close to him, and talk to him," Adam encouraged. "Are you afraid?" I nodded. "Good," he said, "we are getting to the bottom of this."

I crouched down and moved close to Harry. Harry wheeled around to look at me with his dark, piercing gaze. He moved back to nosing dirt over the bone. I moved closer.

"Hey, what's up Harry? Do you need some help here?" I came up beside Harry in his anxious task of covering the bone. Harry looked confused, then relaxed as I joined in gently pawing the dirt over his bone. I moved closer while pushing more dirt. In that moment, Harry's eyes transformed. His fear-clouded eyes became trusting. I was understanding what Harry was doing. I was not being commanding. I was not being demanding. I was not asking Harry to submit to a higher authority. I was communicating that I understood his protective ritual. It was an absolutely spiritual moment of communion.

I searched under the dirt for the bone with one hand while I continued pushing dirt with the other. I found the bone and slowly brought it out. I patted Harry's head and talked to him. Slowly I moved away, and Harry easily and trustingly came with me. It was the most profound communication I have ever had with an animal. I had met Harry where he needed to be understood and where I had failed to understand him time and again. I had showed Harry that I understood his life-and-death need to protect the items he carried around like puppies.

Perhaps at some point in Harry's life before I adopted him he had had to take care of puppies, pawing up shallow "nests" for them, gently nosing them to keep them covered and safe, continually moving them to new safer ground. Why he has the compulsion to continue this behavior with such intensity we will probably never know. But what we can surmise is that Harry has a very great capacity for care, protection, and love.

It was a unique experience in my life. And it highlights the profundity of empathy and its role in love. Empathy, an integral part of love, allows us to deeply understand what another truly needs. By helping Harry with the bone he treated like a treasured puppy, I had finally shown Harry that I understood his story that he had told so many times before without being heard. Like a mother learning to respond to the cues of her infant, we must learn the subtle cues of our animals.

Though it may seem like I'm anthropomorphizing Harry's behavior, watching the transformation in Harry leads me to believe that, whatever transpired (and we shall never truly know), Harry experienced me in a very different way that day. I certainly experienced him in a different way! My fear was replaced by an empathic understanding that paved the way for a deeper relationship.

Empathy and Empathic Deficit

BECAUSE EMPATHY IS such a critical part of love, when it is lacking (what psychotherapists call an "empathic deficit"), love cannot be felt or expressed or accepted fully. Empathetic deficits happen when our "normal" developmental cycle is interrupted and we miss critical experiential learning. Most often, people will replace the critical experiential learning with an intellectual mimicking behavior. For example, I was raised without a mother, though it is not immediately apparent in the way I behave. I learned very quickly to take care of myself, leaping many developmental milestones into a seemingly independent, confident person. At the core of my being, though, there is a person arrested at five years old who lost her mother to a terminal illness. Because I am so adept at camouflaging, even to myself, the holes in my being where the missed experiences should be, it takes these profound crises like being bitten by a dog to uncover what I have missed in life. Fundamentally, I had to relearn how to authentically respect myself, love myself, and locate my deepest intuition to learn to trust myself in order to allow the love that I had not experienced in my early life. Because I had jumped over so many learning experiences in which, rather than having someone taking care of my needs, I was alone to take care of myself, I became adept at ignoring my own needs and noticing the needs of others. I spent far too much time loving others and not paying attention to what was or wasn't coming to me. To this day, it takes a great deal of attention on my part to notice what I need. Though the specifics are different for other people, the process is the same. It is what therapy attempts to redress by providing a safe environment for a person in which to pick up the lost pieces of his or her developmental life, whether through peering into the past or, as in Gestalt therapy, by becoming aware of the present processes and what they reveal to us.

I have a client, Jeannie, who had an empathic deficit that manifested itself in a different way. She seemed unable to care about others and only expressed deep concern for how others cared about her. She was a bottomless pit of need that evidently developed because of a mother who was physically present but emotionally absent, and a father who gave mixed messages of attraction and disdain. As a child, this woman had been chubby and was constantly told she was fat and unattractive. As a woman, she became aggressively assertive towards her friends and boyfriends for not giving her what she needed. She was completely unaware of the impact she had on others and of what others needed from her. She seemed unable to be empathic, to understand anyone else's needs but her own. I am very pleased that this woman is now happily married and is a wonderful mother to her children. The empathic deficit was repaired well enough to allow her a rich and rewarding life that includes the care of others, something she was at one time totally unable to do.

Humans are not the only creatures that can benefit from such emotional repair work. Remember Dr. Prosen from the chapter on trust, and Brian, the bonobo primate he worked with at the Milwaukee Zoo? Dr. Prosen's treatment plan for Brian was to first understand the empathic deficit, then begin to repair the deficit. The mothering of Brian by the old, blind female primate was the first step to providing Brian the opportunity to experience the loving kindness of a mother he had missed during his early years caged with his abusive father.

Another wonderful story from Dr. Prosen's work that illustrates the depth of emotion primates possess is the story of an orangutan named Dick and his lost love. Brian soothed Dick during an extended depression that no one really understood. Through inquiry, Dr. Prosen discovered that Dick had become depressed after he had fractured his arm and his oldest son was paired off with his mate. For ten years, Dick could see his son and his ex-mate living as mates in an adjoining cage. Dick's ten-year depression lifted once he was reunited with his mate.

Until I experienced Harry's episode with nesting, I believed that he too was suffering from an empathic deficit. It now makes sense to me why love alone did not alter his behavior. Harry was not necessarily suffering from an empathic deficit; he was suffering from my lack of empathic observation of his story. Harry is in fact a highly empathic animal, extremely responsive to the moods and cues of those around him. Empathy is what allows us to listen to the stories we are being told and to see them from the perspective of the teller rather than our own. It had been empathy that had allowed Dr. Prosen to observe the orangutan, to listen to the history of his broken arm and the loss of his son and his mate, and to immediately understand Dick's ten-year depression.

Similarly, Adam had watched Harry's gentle nosing of the earth over his bone and immediately understood the aggressive behavior that had stymied us both. I had gotten so caught up in the horror of being bitten that I could not see what Harry had been telling me until I had the guidance of Adam's empathic understanding while I confronted the depth of my fear. Adam believed and trusted both Harry and me enough to know that we could walk those depths. I am forever grateful to have gotten there because of what it revealed about Harry. Empathy is an exceedingly loving act.

There is a Sufi story that illustrates the power of empathy. It is about three old men sitting in a doorway. A man walks past them. One of the seated men says, "That man needs a drink of milk." "How did you know?" the others ask, incredulously. "I was a milkman once. I know that look."

Choosing Love

ONE OF MY FRIENDS takes more care choosing a pair of shoes than choosing a mate. She will shop for days and weeks to find the right pair of shoes in the right color with the right fit to complement her outfit. Each aspect of the shoe is considered for its own merits and for how it relates to her wardrobe. If she considered the men in her life with such care, she may not have been so quick to accept anyone who offered her a shred of attention. This is a woman who is intelligent and also funny, beautiful, financially secure, and independent. It has to be her need for attention that has thus far gotten in the way of finding a responsible partner. By finding an empathic listener to help her heal this lack within herself, she might be able to look deeper when choosing someone with whom real love can develop.

Without understanding ourselves, we don't know why we choose or how we choose the mates we do. I realized one day that my criteria for choosing my men and my dog had been eerily similar — He's seems intelligent! He's really cute! He has a little beard! I love him! One night when I was having dinner with some friends, including Adam Stone, Adam joked with me about my taste in dogs. He had noticed that each dog at his farm for which I had really fallen for has been a hardened little delinquent. He teased me about whether the kinds of dogs I was attracted to were a reflection of the men I had chosen in my life. Though I didn't answer at the time, I believe there is an element of truth to that. With neither man nor beast had I considered, Does he have a history? How does he relate to people, to children — is he hard-spirited or kind and gentle? Do we have similar ideas about how we should live, how we deal with issues?

Had I looked harder when Harry was brought into the adoption booth, I would have realized this dog had history written all over him. He bounced off four walls and couldn't wait to get out of the room, out of the building, out of the street, out of his collar, and out of sight. When I first met Harry, as when I first meet a man, I tended to look only at what was wonderful about him and not at what else his behavior suggested.

If I had known then — when I first adopted Harry — what I know now, I may not have adopted him. Though I do not now regret for a moment adopting Harry. I am far more interested in the process of life than in being concerned with predicting and controlling outcomes. The sense of surprise of what life brings even when the surprise is sometimes painful or disturbing is far more meaningful for me than living with predictability. It is in the process of allowing events to unfold naturally that love either grows or it doesn't.

My friend, Cindy, has a saying, "When you go to a restaurant, you look for a clean table, don't you? Why not look for a clean table when you are looking for a partner?" So many people begin relationships without a clean table. Those relationships will have so much clutter, so much left over stuff from previous "dinners," it will be difficult to clean it up along the way. Not impossible (for those of you who just gasped), just more difficult.

What is a clean table in a relationship? One that begins in a state of integrity, that is, where both parties feel whole, where we have thought about, understood, learned from, and feel finished with issues from our previous relationships so that we can be open (clean) for the new one. Many of us can probably think of a relationship that began without that state of integrity, and the lack of which has led to its eventual demise. Regaining lost integrity is extremely difficult, but when you do it, it clears the table. To regain integrity you must think about all those people in your life with whom you have unfinished business — left over resentments, bitterness, or anger. Decide what unfinished business you can deal with — the more the better — and begin to make peace. There are some things that you may regret doing or saying that you may just have to accept, but there are many things that you can do through honest communication with true intention to clear up a misunderstanding, unresolved hurt, resentment, or bitterness with others. It is very difficult to move forwards in relationships when one or the other remains burdened with an unfinished past.

When thinking about a potential love partner, we need to ask ourselves, What is this person's baggage? What is the core quality of the person? How does he or she deal with me when there is a problem? Are we able to discuss things rationally? Does this person give respect? Does he or she listen? Do I want to understand this person and does he or she want to understand me? Can I be myself with this person and respect this person, and can I maintain that when the going gets tough?

If we meet someone and our immediate thought is this person is great and once he or she changes this, that, or the other thing, things will be amazing, we may as well stop deluding ourselves. We are seeing someone for who we want them to be, not for who they are.

Successful Love

WHAT IS SUCCESSFUL love? Is it a long-term commit-
ted relationship that doesn't end until death do us part? Is it a loving, respectful relationship that may not last forever, but while it
does last is wonderful, enriching, and meaningful? Is it a success
to stay in a problem relationship and work on a solution? Even if
there are few returns? Or is it success to end a problem relationship, setting each partner free to find a more fulfilling life? I don't
believe there is one answer. For some, it may be pushing through
difficult situations and remaining through the loveless times with
a partner, creating an enduring bond. For others, it may be characterized by relationships where the love is palpable, can traverse
challenges, but may not endure.

As in the writing of this book, where on a daily basis the work
evolves, my thinking evolves, and consequently the words on the
page change, relationships change and evolve. Nothing is true forever, unless it is.

Solid Loving

AT THE COTTAGE our family rented this summer, my
brother, Nick, came up with his friends Chris and Julie and their
five-month-old baby, Trinity. Julie is a young mother but it was
incredible to see how solid she was. She is extremely loving and
also completely capable of allowing Trinity to find her own experiences. Julie, as a mother, is not overly solicitous of her child. Julie
seemed to be the embodiment of D.W. Winnicott's theory I discussed earlier of the "good enough" mother without ever having
heard about the theory. Julie put Trinity in the Jolly Jumper inside
the cottage and played with her lovingly. Once Trinity was happily
jumping around, Julie came outside to join us. She stayed outside
just a few minutes, then went back inside and talked to Trinity.
Julie came back outside and stayed with us for a longer period of

time. Then Julie went to the door and called a few loving words to Trinity. We could hear Trinity nattering and giggling to herself. Julie said she wanted Trinity to have the experience of being on her own but knowing that her mother would come back to her. Julie also said she needed time away from Trinity and liked to know that she could leave Trinity for a few minutes alone and not feel panicked by it.

Julie unknowingly articulated the kernel of Winnicott's teachings, and it seems to be integral to what a child needs to develop an internal core of solid love and security. What I love about the way Julie mothers is that there is nothing romanticized about it. She is being a mother and she is being Julie. If, as I think they will, Julie and Chris are able to adapt to each stage of their child's life as well as they do now, I suspect that Trinity will grow up to be a very solid person.

When we discover our own sense of security — as Julie was giving to Trinity — we do not look towards others to provide our happiness, our well-being, or our sense of purpose. We allow freedom for ourselves and for the people we are in relationships with to be exactly who they are. I had a relationship with a man I love and respect very much. I was very sad when the relationship ended before he moved back to Europe. We spent sometime afterwards talking about our relationship and how we felt about each other. He said to me one day with surprise, "Why are you so happy when we had such a sad time last week breaking up?" I told him I was still very sad we were no longer together romantically, but that my essential happiness did not depend on him.

Romanticizing and Expectations

I TALK ABOUT expectations many times throughout this book because I believe that unfulfilled expectations are what generate a lot of our difficulties in life. We are so busy expecting things to be a certain way, to evolve a certain way, that we lose the ability to handle life just the way it happens. It happened I adopted a street dog that would not be forgiving of my dysfunctional leadership. However, he would be forever forgiving and deeply loving if I learned from those experiences. Similarly, letting go of unrealistic expectations and accepting our loved ones the way they are allows us to create better and more fulfilling relationships based on mutual courage, trust, respect, and love.

Jeffrey Moussaieff Masson, whose writings I love, says, "Humans confuse love and adoration with entitlement." I tend to agree with him and find that what arises from that are people looking to their friends, partners, children, and even their dogs to fulfill their own needs. I found an example of this in an article by Colin Muncie, which I recently read in the monthly magazine *Health Watch*. Muncie suggested, "If you yearn to be unconditionally loved get a dog. But a dog is good not only for your ego but for your health, mental and physical." I agree that dogs are good for you, but I think that yearning for unconditional love is the wrong reason to get a dog. Rather, if you have love to give, get a dog. We need to look at dogs as living beings that deserve respect and our love. It is our human arrogance that tends to look at others and animals for what we can get from them, rather than what we can give. We risk treating our dogs as our possessions, disposable, easily gotten rid of if they displease us or take up too much of our time. Our dogs, our pets, our animals are a commitment we need to take seriously to maintain our humanity.

Romanticized Love

DR. MARK BEKOFF writes in his article "Dog Trust: Deep Lessons in Compassion, Devotion, Respect, Spirituality, and Love from our Loving Companions," "Their wide eyes that pierce our souls tell us clearly that they just know we'll always do the best we can for them ... their innate, ancestral, and deep faith in us, their unwavering belief that we will take our responsibilities to them as seriously as we assume responsibility for other humans." Unfortunately, Harry did not possess that innate, ancestral deep faith in humankind that Bekoff writes of. Harry did not innately trust me or any other human, and I had to learn how to breach that gulf in our relationship.

The problem with the attitude that dogs are all trust, love, and compassion is that it romanticizes dogs in much the same way that movies romanticize human love. It provides us with unrealistic expectations. No wonder there are so many people out in the world feeling like failures because their dogs will not come to them. We believe it must be because there is something wrong with us, since we have been taught to think that dogs will automatically be perfect companions. Or it means that there is a defect in our particular dog because he doesn't fit our expectations. Don't get me wrong; I believe strongly that dogs have perhaps even a greater capacity than humans for trust, love, compassion, and certainly devotion, but this doesn't necessarily come prepackaged in the animal. Often it must be developed through patient understanding, empathy, and a deep and abiding respect.

Likewise, when we look to our romantic relationships for unconditional love, we are often attempting to recreate our first mother-infant bond rather than creating a mature loving exchange between two adults. By looking at our relationships and the style and manner in which we love, we can learn so much about ourselves and how we romanticize love. It takes an honest appraisal of how we love. Do we love selflessly? Do we then feel taken advantage of? Not all of us are as evolved as the Dalai Lama to be able to achieve a state of being where our love is authentically selfless. My friend, Evelyn, the psychologist I mentioned previously, constantly challenges what she jokingly calls my "altruistic intentions in relationships." I have to think deeply about what I am feeling, what I expect — if anything — in return, and if I don't expect anything, why I don't. Healthy love requires us to give and take.

On the other hand, we can also ask ourselves, do we love sparingly? Do we then feel that love is never enough? There is so much we can learn when we begin to look at the circumstances of our relationships. We expect that love will fill us even when we are unwilling to give very much of ourselves. Oprah Winfrey says, "Happiness is never something you get from other people. The happiness you feel is in direct proportion to the love you give." It is extraordinarily difficult to have a loving relationship when every act must fill an unfillable void. I have worked with many such people in my practice. Their concern is always with themselves and what they are not receiving. These people feel profoundly deprived and are constantly on the lookout for being taken advantage of. They see others as selfish, as not wanting to give, but these feelings towards others are merely projections of their own desperate needs. It is a kind of emotional greediness that once realized can eventually be transformed into emotional giving — after the core deprivation has been taken care of.

Does your child walk all over you now that he or she is a teen? Does your spouse take you for granted? Do you take your spouse for granted? Do people always seem to be doing for you, or are you always doing for others? Do you do for others because you worry they might not love you otherwise? Do you worry about your spouse being at home when you are out with your friends? Are you out with your friends every night? Or once a week? Do you know how your spouse feels about it? Are you worrying for nothing because you feel undeserving or insecure? Have you made yourself no longer care how others feel? What do we expect from our closest relationships and what do our loved ones expect of us? We need to continue asking ourselves the hard questions in life, otherwise we will never do what we need to do to change things.

In the Name of Love

SO MUCH IS DONE IN the name of love and not all of it worthy of praise. Conventional wisdom says love is supposed to be natural, something we don't have to know much about, think much about, do much about. We have children, they love us, we love them. We have pets, they love us, we love them. We have parents, they love us, we love them. If only it were that simple. We are complex beings and what may have been natural thousands of years ago has gotten quite complicated. How do we reconcile what we think love should be with what love often is?

I worked with a woman whose parents were Holocaust survivors. They loved their only child and in the name of that love they protected her from everything they thought might be painful to her. Their intent was loving but the effects were ultimately damaging. The woman was protected and pampered and given everything material that life had to offer. The importance of appearance was emphasized. She lived a Barbie-doll existence. She was blond, cute, and had a figure that even Barbie would envy. But she felt empty inside. The Barbie-doll existence was a barren one. Her parents unwittingly robbed her of her own true experiences because of their experiences in concentration camps. In the name of love they did not ever want their beautiful daughter to suffer as they had.

For years, the woman was unable to create deep and lasting bonds with men, as she had no experience with the painful realities of developing a bond. When her relationships began to get difficult, she immediately bailed out. She had been so protected that she did not know how to traverse the depths of a human personality, her own or someone else's. Everything for her was kept light and airy, simple and nonthreatening. She may have been able to live a life as a Barbie-doll wife for a man who didn't want more than that, but she happened to also have been blessed (or cursed) with a fine intellect. She knew there was more to life than a fine gossamer veil of niceness and pleasantness.

The woman experienced a smiling depression. She smiled because she could not do otherwise. To do otherwise was to acknowledge that there was pain and suffering in the world, things she had been forbidden to learn about. As the depression ate away at the edges of her smile, she sought therapy in an effort to eradicate the depression. What she found instead was her soul — deep, compassionate, very loving, and sometimes deeply affected by the sadness around her.

How We Confuse Love

A FRIEND OF MINE is a bright, successful, beautiful single woman. She has struggled for the past few years asking herself difficult questions so she can understand her behavior patterns and the behavior of the men she dates. She told me that she recognized something very important recently. She described how she goes along in life for a while and then begins to think to herself, wouldn't it be nice to have someone who would share some of her difficulties. She said it is a short hop to that once unconscious feeling of wanting to be saved and looking for someone to save her. She began laughing as she told me this and said, "I'm looking to be saved and then inevitably I meet someone. I think I've found love, when really what I've found is a jerk not looking to save me but to save himself." She said she is finally realizing that she doesn't need to be saved.

I think this confusion happens often. We think we are looking for love, but we are looking for some other need to be filled. We do the reverse as well. We might think we need to overeat, but what we are really needing is love. We think we need to buy things, but we really need love. We think we need to drink, but what we need is to love and be loved.

Who Are You

MAYA ANGELOU SAID, "When people show you who they are, believe them." The simplicity of these words belies their depth. Some of us tend to believe what people say they are rather than believe what their actions show us they are. I have found that most people show us who they are fairly quickly in the relationship, and it is only when we have our eyes and our minds open to our perceptions that we are able to understand this. We need to learn how to distinguish the personality from the character of a person. Many smooth and charismatic personalities conceal an unsavory character. The sad man who describes himself as the victim of the ex-wife who left him may be emotionally unavailable and may have behaved in ways that led to the demise of their relationship. When we stay blind to the signs in front of us, we can believe in a love that doesn't exist. The confident business woman who acts independent and witty might actually feel bitter and be guarded in her relationships. The behavior of a person reveals everything. Pay attention to your instincts. A person who cannot answer questions in a straightforward manner might have something to hide. When you know who you are, you will know who others are, echoes the words of my friend. Seeing ourselves clearly helps us see others clearly.

Where Love Grows

LOVE IS FORGED IN those tiny moments where we least expect it. Love grows when it is challenged and the challenge is successfully navigated. Love deepens when we find empathy for another. Love flourishes when we have an open heart and an open mind. Love develops when we take a courageous stand, trust in ourselves or someone else, and respect others.

When Harry resists me and I find a way to push through his resistance and gain his trust, our love deepens. When I finally understood Harry's bone-burying behavior, love flourished. Our relationship was challenged in the most fundamental way when he bit me, and it was the decision to hang in and understand what had gone wrong that produced a genuine transformation in both Harry and me.

My stepdaughter was a challenge for the first few years we lived together. By successfully navigating Sarah's multitude of tests, our relationship developed and our love grew as our fear and suspicion of each other subsided. As I look back on the years Sarah and I spent together, I can recognize the cornerstones of healing in action. We have been courageous in the way we have communicated with each other, we developed trust and a deep respect for each other, and our love continues.

When in Northern Ireland with Cindy Wasser, a criminal lawyer and, on my invitation, a member of the international observer delegation to the North of Ireland, we were to be billeted with a wonderful local couple, Sean and Maria. Cindy arrived, with several of the local youths carrying her enormous suitcases for her. The luggage filled Sean and Maria's living room. I had already arrived, carrying a backpack, and I cringed when I saw Cindy, feeling I had made a huge mistake by inviting her. I wondered how I could share a month in Ireland with someone who was so obviously oblivious to what the delegation was all about. And now I was going to have to share bunkbeds with her in a closet-sized child's room.

The experience, however, cemented our friendship. During cold rainy days and damp rainy nights, we shared observation posts, watching the conflict in the six counties unfold before us in the microcosm of the 12th of July marching parade, listening to the personal stories of systematic discrimination and oppression, and interviewing government officials and leaders. Together we faced danger from a hostile security force, we faced boredom through long nights on lonely watches, we faced the disdain of some locals and the acceptance of others. Cindy was not who I initially thought her to be. She was strong, feisty, quick-witted, analytical, deep, and incredibly intelligent. Our love for each other as friends grew through the challenges of sharing such close quarters during extreme conditions with too little sleep and too much coffee, during extremely emotionally tense times.

It is hard to imagine the intensity of being part of a human rights delegation during such politically explosive times as the 12th of July marching parades in Northern Ireland. The tension among the residents is palpable, the possibility of violence is ever present, and the heightened awareness for conflict is emotionally taxing. The reality is worse. Cindy and I went on several delegations, and the last time we were there together, three young children were burned to death in their home in a fire caused by a petrol bomb.

By the time the delegation was over, Cindy's suitcases became the source of many of our jokes, and the woman I at one time couldn't imagine sharing a moment with has become one of my closest friends. Sean and Maria were to become our lifetime friends as well. They embraced me as one of their own and took me on their family vacation to Donegal, where Sean gave me a historical tour of the country. At Drogha Na'Neor — the Bridge of Tears — we shed tears for the three children who were killed in the house fire and made a wish over the bridge that peace would come soon. Love is present when we share the sadness for the tragic loss of others, and sharing that moment with Sean, Maria, and their three children will stay with me forever.

Too Much Love

CAN YOU LOVE TOO much? Is it genuine love if you are giving too much? Is giving too much perhaps a function of not enough mutuality? How can much love be too much? The answer lies in the nature of the love itself. Love should bring out the best in both partners. When a relationship is destructive to either partner (for example, when one partner loses his or her sense of self in giving to the other), it is not love that is at fault but the expression of a more destructive emotion such as fear, lack of trust, or lack of respect. There was a popular book a few years back titled, *Women Who Love too Much*. It chronicled women who loved men at the expense of themselves and their self-respect. Love needs to be centered between the self and other.

Given how our lives can be shaped by fear and love, and how our experiences of love are shaped by our lives, it isn't surprising that many of us learn about love from our dogs. There is so much to learn about love. This story came from the book *Motherless Daughters*, by Hope Edelman: "[I] all of a sudden realized I could be furious at my dog and still love him ... You know that you can mess up ... and they'll still love you and won't try to take you back to the pound ... letting myself risk love and letting myself be loved, is one of the biggest challenges left for me."

Love Is Elemental

WHY SHOULD SOMETHING as elemental as love be such a huge challenge for so many? A friend recently told me a story about visiting her sister, happily married for twenty years with two boys, one of whom is a particular challenge, as he has ADHD (attention deficit hyperactivity disorder). After watching her sister and brother-in-law in a vehement argument, my friend asked her sister how she could say such horrible things to her husband. Her sister said matter of factly, "He's my husband. If we can't be our ugliest with each other, then who can we be ugly with?"

This made an impression on my friend, who is beautiful, bright, intelligent, and divorced. She has spent her past relationships being on her best behavior in an effort to win love, yet never really experiencing love. She has not yet felt that she is innately worthy of being fully and completely loved for who she is, though this is changing for her. She is beginning to be aware of herself, and she is beginning to know what kind of relationship she wants and what kind of person she will be able to have it with.

There is no doubt that I love my dog. Some of my friends express surprise that I could love him after he bit me. I would not have tolerated continued biting, but since I did love him, I gathered my courage and went searching for the knowledge I needed to change his behavior and our relationship. When it became clear that Harry was responding to my confusion rather than being just plain vicious, a relationship with him became possible.

The other day, a friend and I took our dogs to the woods for a walk. Brian is blessed with a difficult, large German shepherd. Shadow showed up on Brian's doorstep one day and never left. Shadow's claim to fame is his penchant for running in the opposite direction to which he is called. Shadow will run for miles. It is quite likely that is how he got lost in the first place and ended up at Brian's farm. Brian has been working with Shadow for a while now, as I have with Harry. We share our small victories and our frustrations. Recently Brian said he realized something about his relationship with Shadow that echoed all his other relationships. He had been treating Shadow's training as though it were an obligation, a task to be driven to completion, a task not to be enjoyed but endured. Slowly Brian's enjoyment of his relationship with his dog had lost its energy and turned into solemn duty. Neither was very happy.

I understand how easily that can happen, as it happens often with Harry and happens often with human relationships. A sense of duty gets superimposed onto what is enjoyment and soon the passion to be together seeps away. When Harry is particularly stubborn, I get frustrated with him and I take on my training with a fervor that could extinguish any love on any side. I try to remember what happened with Brian and what has happened to me in my past relationships, where passions have given way to tired, energyless obligations. Love is like doors, thresholds to be walked through again and again and again. Enjoyment, passion, and fun keep love alive, and duty, obligation, and lack of communication poison love.

There is no greater fulfillment than that of love — the love of life, of others, of animals, and of ourselves when that love is born out of courage, trust, and respect. When we authentically love, we bring a greater sense of compassion and responsibility into our lives and the world, and our actions are guided by loving principles. A friend sent me a story — it seems to be an old fable, though I don't know where the story originated — that illustrates the power of love.

A woman came out of her house and saw three old men with long white beards sitting in her front yard. She did not recognize them. She said, "I don't think I know you, but you must be hungry. Please come in and have something to eat." "Is the man of the house home they asked?" "No," she said, "He is out." "Then we cannot come in," they replied.

In the evening when her husband came home, she told him what had happened. "Go tell them I am home and invite them in." The woman went out and invited the men in. "We do not go into a house together," they replied. "Why is that?" she wanted to know. One of the old men explained. "His name is Wealth," he said, pointing to one of his friends, and pointing to another one, "He is success, and I am Love." Then he added, "Now go in and discuss with your husband which one of us you want in your home."

The woman went in and told her husband what was said. Her husband was overjoyed. "How nice!" he said, "Since that is the case, let us invite Wealth. Let him come and fill our home with wealth!" His wife disagreed. "My dear, why don't we invite Success?" Their daughter was listening from the other corner of the house. She jumped in with her own suggestion. "Would it not be better to invite Love? Our home will then be filled with love!"

"Let us heed our daughter's advice," said the husband to his wife. "Go out and invite Love to be our guest." The woman went out and asked the three old men, "Which one of you is Love? Please come in and be our guest." Love got up and started walking towards the house. The other two also got up and followed him. Surprised, the lady asked Wealth and Success, "I only invited Love. Why are you coming in?" The old men replied together, "If you had invited Wealth or Success, the other two of us would have stayed out, but since you invited Love, wherever he goes, we go with him. Wherever there is Love, there is also Wealth and Success."

LESSONS IN LOVE

- Nurture yourself to maintain your resources for nurturing others.
- Recognize that different temperaments have different needs.
- Become aware of your inner feelings and empathic deficits that need healing to fully open to love.
- Be patient when building genuine love.
- Be aware of what's left on a "table" to clean up.
- When you don't choose a "clean table," recognize that you must clear off the unfinished business in order to move forward.
- Decide for yourself what constitutes successful love, but be careful not to justify someone else's lack of respect for you or your own lack of self-respect.
- Discover your own sense of security and don't look to others to provide your happiness.
- Let go of unrealistic expectations and accept your loved ones for who they are.
- Continually ask yourself the difficult questions so that you know how to change things for the better.
- Accept that sadness and pain are part of life.
- Save yourself.
- Be open to what people's actions tell you about themselves.

The Lessons Continue

And when old words die out on the tongue, new melodies break forth from the heart, and where the old tracks are lost, new country is revealed with its wonders.

— RABINDRONATH TAGORE GITANJALI

JUST WHEN IT SEEMS I have learned so much, I discover that there is yet another deeper layer to uncover. My journey with Harry continues to this day and my lessons are beginning to take on the flavor of a weekly koan (Zen riddle) to decipher. Adam Stone's twenty-eight-day program to reform aggressive dogs is just an introduction leading to the deeper aspects of communicating and understanding my dog and dog behavior. Twenty-eight days have turned into a year, and a small group of us continue with our learning, breaking through times when we hated ourselves, hated our dogs, and hated Adam. How could any of us have imagined that this journey could go on for so long and that we could create with our dogs a communication so profound?

When I first began this journey with Harry, it was merely to eradicate the unwanted aggression in my dog. The journey was pragmatic. The journey had a destination. The elements of healing were simply a method to organize the lessons I was learning. But the journey has become something more akin to a spiritual awakening, where every element of my life becomes another door to open. As the deepening of communication with Harry continues, I find the model of the four elements of healing more and more powerful in day-to-day life.

In my practice I find the four elements of healing an effective model for guiding people in their relationships with themselves and others, leading to a deeper, more meaningful, life. When one looks at situations and issues, the specifics are always different, but the process of navigating through the issues almost always requires one or more or a combination of the elements. We need courage to face difficult obstacles that we fear; we need to develop some trust either in ourselves or in someone else; we need to respect ourselves or others; and when dealing with love, courage, trust, and respect are integral issues. The elements offer some clarity and simplicity to complex, seemingly indecipherable, issues.

For example, I had a client who was struggling with how to proceed with the next phase of his career. He was up for a senior executive position — not a CEO position but one that was certainly financially secure, prestigious, and would be considered an excellent career move — yet he felt some reluctance that he couldn't quite get a handle on. The more he thought about things, the more confused he became, and of course everyone he spoke to had a different angle on advice to give. He had given the company scenario some thought and had hit upon an idea of creating a unique position that would benefit everyone in the company and which made him excited about joining the company. Yet, he hadn't trusted his intuition that his strategy was not just a good one but an excellent one. He feared losing the offered position if he raised a different possibility for himself, all the while not really wanting the job that had been offered. After we talked, my client realized that by trusting his instincts and finding a little courage, he could put forward his idea. If his idea was accepted, the position would excite and challenge him. If his idea wasn't accepted, he realized that he would never be happy with the position as it had been created.

In my personal life I have begun to appreciate the depth of the cornerstones. The way that courage, trust, respect, and love affect my relationships and the way I live my life is profound. I consciously use the cornerstones of healing as mental hooks in my life to guide my actions and reactions.

In my current relationships, whenever I feel disturbed about something and consequently become quiet, I remind myself about having the courage to become aware of what my true feelings are and to speak up about my truth. With courage as my guide, I have taken chances in my relationships that I may not have otherwise. By courageously speaking up, my relationships have become much deeper, more open and honest. Or they end more quickly, which is preferable to me than a long drawn-out process whereby things are left unsaid and issues left not raised. The people in my life experience the difference in my approach, and they are inspired to respond in kind.

The elements build upon each other. I find that the courageous communication I practice is creating more trust in my relationships. I trust myself more because I am searching internally to discover my own experience. The more I make it my habit to become aware of my perceptions and feelings, the more I am able to express myself clearly and honestly. I stay aware of how I am behaving and how others are behaving. This leads to greater trust and authenticity in my relationships and therefore greater intimacy.

Without respect, relationships flounder and eventually fail. We cannot expect someone else to respect us if we don't first respect ourselves. This has been a particularly difficult and paradoxical lesson for me, one that I must remain constantly aware of. Through learning to build respect in my relationship with Harry,

I learned how tenuous my self-respect had been. I learned to value myself, to continually remind myself of the way I desire my relationships to be, and to not settle for anything less, while at the same time respecting someone else's desires that may not be in harmony with my own.

   With the foundations of courage, trust, and respect, love has the possibility to flourish and succeed. For almost two years, I pushed through the difficulties of developing a relationship with a problem dog. I am persistent, if nothing else. The rewards are rich. I dug through to the core of Harry and learned so much about myself, relationships, and authentic love. In searching for the core of Harry, I found my own core and what I am truly capable of. The elements of healing keep delivering their lessons in ever-deepening ways. As in the Taoist martial art, ba gua chang, deep lessons never seem to end. In ba gua chang, you walk the circle — a practice that exists in many cultures and a seemingly simple concept. But as a practice, it centers the mind and the soul in continuous circular and unpredictable movements that cultivate and use energy, developing the physical, emotional, mental, and spiritual domains. The actions may seem simple to an observer but, as an inner practice, there is endless refining of the movements that leads to an understanding of the deeper aspects of its spiritual nature. It can be profound. My teacher says that ba gua is a practice of opening the heart. I believe that any practice that opens the heart is a practice worth cultivating in a world short on love, tolerance, and compassion. Love is not just about loving a partner, though ultimately that is what most of us desire. Love is about loving everything: life, others, animals, and the planet. The Dalai Lama says, "Love for others and respect for their rights and dignity, no matter who or what they are: ultimately these are all we need ... compassion is what makes our life meaningful. It is the source of all lasting happiness and joy ... happiness is inextricably bound up with the happiness of others. There is no denying that if society suffers, we ourselves suffer."

Midnight Walks and Talks

ON OUR FIRST MIDNIGHT off-leash walk, our group of guru dogs walked down the country road where Adam lives. It was part of a no-talk exercise that had been going on for several weeks. We were not to verbally communicate to our dogs, communicating only with our minds and our bodies. In the dark it took on new meaning. We had to trust that our dogs would find a way to walk along with us, not run away, not get lost, not get into a dog fight. Each of us had our own demons to exorcise. Mine was that Harry would stray too deep into the fields or play too aggressively, someone else's was that her dog would attack, and another's was that his dog would run away. We walked. The sky was black and filled with stars. The land was flat agricultural land; the empty road seemed to stretch on forever. A single light from the next farm shone in the distance. The wheat fields glowed in the dark, and I was sure they would seduce Harry into their depths with their other-worldly allure.

Adam slipped up beside me and asked me to listen for Harry. He said listen for his sounds, his breathing, his walking, his heartbeat. He said we should always be like one, no matter how close or far away from each other we are. In the darkness I could hear all the dogs, then I began to be able to distinguish Harry's tags clinking as he trotted along. I found I could recognize his gait as distinct from the others. He was closer to me than I thought. Adam told me that is how close we now are. I needed to trust it. To trust Harry and to trust our bond. I could hear his tags, I could hear his panting, I could even hear his pads on the gravel road, but I sure couldn't hear his heartbeat ... yet.

Jennifer and I often had long talks between our sessions about what we were learning about our dogs, our relationships, and ourselves. We questioned and challenged everything and each other. Was this what Adam meant? Did he not say something different before? I don't like what he is saying here. I think it is this way. I think it is that way. I am confused.

Confusion is the state before real learning occurs. In Gestalt therapy, it is the state when the old figure/ground (how you perceive the foreground and background of an issue) begins to break up to form a new figure, a new gestalt, a new wholeness. Confusion is what I experienced when I began the practice of ba gua chang. Now I live in a state of perpetual "not-knowing." It is comforting in an odd sort of way. It is the beginning of a state of spontaneity, where one no longer has to anticipate or control events that are really not within the realm of our control anyway. It is a state of trusting yourself to know what to do, or not do. And either state is fine.

What Jennifer and I learned during our talks was that we both had a propensity towards working things out verbally, questioning and challenging each other's understanding and the teaching we were learning. Jennifer had been a dog trainer, therefore her dog skills were well beyond my own. I enjoyed her experience in our talks. We could begin with a simple question, neither one of us wedded to any particular outcome, weave our way through many paths, and discover something at the end. Often we found that we were trying to imitate the way Adam did something with the dogs instead of finding our own style. We kept learning that lesson week after week.

Adam had a very commanding way of doing things. When we tried to imitate him, we came off like dominatrixes, instead of being ourselves. Jennifer's Buddy and my Harry were similar in that they cannot abide inauthenticity. If Jennifer was not herself, Buddy, a one-hundred-and-forty-pound rotty crossed with a Tibetan mastiff, lay down, refused to move, and growled his displeasure. Harry would engage me in a power struggle and use his speed and strength to make me look like a fool. The lessons go deeper and deeper. We discovered we were blaming Adam for our propensities, memories, or fears of being ineffective, and we turned subtle learning into obedience lessons of power and dominance. We interpreted teaching our dogs to crawl as an obedience lesson instead of realizing that we were the ones making it so rather than making it the lesson in trust it was meant to be. It is a human dilemma to blame another for our shortcomings.

Our Shared Journey

HARRY AND I SHARE A journey. The first part of it has been long and arduous for both of us, but not without its rewards. We have learned many lessons and those lessons keep returning in deeper and deeper forms. I have learned it is not about having to fix yourself or change what you feel is wrong with yourself. It is about learning to accept yourself for who you are but not being limited by who you think you are. It is about deciding what you want in life and how you want to get there. It is about dreaming the impossible and doing what it takes to get there. I had no ability to train a difficult dog when I began this journey, but I envisioned the kind of relationship that I wanted and worked hard towards achieving it. I let go of unrealistic expectations along the way but maintained my original purpose: to have a great relationship with a wonderful dog.

I do not learn my lessons easily. I have never been very accepting of myself. I have always wished that I were taller, had straight hair, were prettier, smarter, and wiser, and I really wish I were funny. I have had to experience my lessons ad nauseam until they are deeply imbedded in my psyche.

I recognize the process in so many areas of my life. Harry is resistant to learning something new and I immediately feel that there is something I am not doing right. I feel that if I were better, Harry wouldn't resist. Sounds crazy when it is stated in black and white, doesn't it? Now I catch myself at the beginning of the process and remember that new learning is often difficult for people (and dogs) and it has little or nothing to do with me. Just as I had learned when I first began doing therapy, I try to go with the resistance to create the change. When you sense resistance in your client, you go with it, rather than against it. As a therapist, you explore the resistance as a creative expression of what the client is experiencing in his or her life, something to become aware of, not something that needs to be torn down, attacked, or eradicated. You are taught to use the resistance to push through to a new understanding.

There is a wonderful Sufi story that illustrates the journey that Harry and I have experienced.

In the mountains a cloud released its contents and a river was born. It flowed down the side of the mountain, through the valley onto the desert, where the river tried to cross but just disappeared into the sand. The river stopped and asked what it should do. The sky said, "Allow me to absorb you and I will take you across the desert."

The river replied, "If I allow you to absorb me then I will no longer be a river." The sky countered, "If you do not allow me to absorb you then you will be no more anyway." This troubled the river. It liked being a river and could not imagine itself as anything different. But try as it might, it could not cross the desert and lost more and more of itself in the sand.

Finally the river relented and allowed itself to be absorbed by the sky. The sky became a powerful wind and whipped over the desert to the other side, where another mountain range began. In the mountains a cloud began to form and soon it became so full, it poured itself onto a mountain, forming a large river that flowed again.

This story depicts how we fear change and tenaciously grip our fragile sense of ourselves, not recognizing that we are capable of transforming without losing our essence. Surrender is the essence of love. We can surrender ourselves and not lose ourselves in the process. We can be water in a river, we can be the air, the wind, become a cloud and be reconstituted in a downpouring of rain. By holding onto ourselves in one context, we can threaten our very existence, like the river at the desert's edge.

Compassion

I WAS WALKING DOWN the street with Harry when a man shuffled towards us. One side of his body was uncooperative, probably the result of a stroke. He stopped in front of us and Harry sat down beside him. The man heaved his clawlike hand on Harry's head to pat him. Harry stood perfectly still and looked up into the man's face with absolute patience. The man continued to clumsily pat Harry's head. He said with his fractured voice, "Nice dog. Very nice dog." Harry looked up at him and seemed to stand a little prouder. I smiled and agreed. I swelled with pride in Harry.

Later that same day, I bought a bottle of wine. A street-lady stood outside the store as I was driving away. I thought that if I had enough money to buy a bottle of wine, I had enough to help an old woman stranded on the street. I stopped the car and held out some change for her from the window. The woman accepted the small amount of change I had and asked if she could pat my dog. Harry nuzzled her hand as she patted him. She broke into a huge toothless smile and said, "Thank you so much for allowing me to touch your dog." The authentic joy that she received from just touching Harry for that brief moment was deeply moving. It is those special moments when Harry can bring such pleasure to a person whose life is so obviously compromised by physical or emotional handicap that makes the work I have done with him so worthwhile.

In God's Time ...

I RECEIVED A STORY sent en masse via e-mail. Usually I delete these e-mails without opening them, but for some reason I read this one. Embedded in the story was a translation of the Greek version of the Bible differentiating two words for time. One is "chronos," which is chronological or linear time, the other is "kairos," which is roughly translated as "in God's time," or "at the right time."

The lessons I learned from Harry came to me at the right time. For the first time in my life, I had the ability to learn from my lessons. I didn't hide from them, I didn't deny them; I kept on learning from them until I got it, and continue getting it. I have been at times a bit lazy and certainly not detail oriented, but these lessons captivated me in a way that made it possible for me to be dedicated and committed.

Power to Inspire

I REALLY BELIEVE THAT we can reinvent ourselves by reaching beyond what we think we are capable of. I think of Sandra Bernhard, who, despite her feeling (and the reality) that she was not a classic beauty, recreated herself through sheer belief and determination as a sexy woman, becoming a cover girl, a runway model, a Playboy bunny, as well as an actress and a comedian. If she had limited herself, she would never have been able to defy the conventional notions of beauty. What I love is that she did it by not buying into the limits of convention. The power of her belief caused others to see her in ways beyond what might have been expected.

Terry Fox, the famous Canadian who ran across the country with one artificial leg while dying of cancer, is another example of an ordinary man who rose to the challenge of achieving something extraordinary and of not limiting what he could accomplish by his physical limitations. There are thousands and thousands of less well-known stories of people who have picked themselves up from the most miserable of circumstances and not allowed it to limit them.

I am honored to have Hillevi as my friend. She had suffered much of her life from a debilitating learning disorder, an abusive father, and a weak, silent mother. For years Hillevi lived on welfare at the fringes of destitution. At the age of forty-something, she lost fifty pounds, got her black belt in tae kwon-do, and began her own business cleaning houses. She is an example of what raw courage and incredible fortitude can do to transform a life. Today, Hillevi is an active member at the Dragonz Martial Arts Centre, volunteering her time to help other adults achieve their dreams of becoming black belts. She smiles with confidence and surrounds herself with positive people who have a positive impact.

What Others Have Learned

WHILE I WAS WRITING this book, many friends, acquaintances, and others who heard about it began writing to me with what they have learned from their life lessons. Here are a few of their stories. I wish I could have included them all, but perhaps they will find their way into another book.

One of my dear friends, Vivien, wrote to me about her current passion, the Argentine tango. I immediately asked her if I could include her story in my book. Vivien vividly captures the essence of passion and the learning process. Her story is about love and the courage to learn something new even when you are not very good at it. It is about having the courage to find your true passions. When you embrace courage as Vivien has done with the tango, the possibility of dreams fulfilled becomes a reality.

LIFELONG YEARNING

Longing, loving, letting go, and the dance of the divine.

I just recently fell in love, passionately, obsessively — with dancing, and more specifically, with the Argentine tango. Now, a friend of mine said, "Well, that's not very useful, is it?" Meaning there are not a lot of people out there in social settings who can do it. But learning the Argentine tango is not about utility, it is about passion, and passion never concerns itself with practicality. It only concerns itself with living life fully.

I was thinking about the topic of lifelong learning, but typed lifelong yearning, and thought, Oh, now that can't be right. But then, what if, in a new-thought, Freudian-slip, hip kind of way, I was thinking about what it really is for me — lifelong learning as a lifelong process of yearning, always reaching towards and retreating from that which fills me, enriches me, and connects me to the Divine.

"Yearning" is the wordless longing that comes over me when I hear tango music. I want to weep. I am immeasurably touched. I see myself dancing in ways I cannot describe, never mind do. And yet, I feel this movement inside me that is Argentine tango, calling me to discover it, to express it. It could just as easily be learning to weave baskets, breed Abyssinian cats, or play mah-jongg, but something, something, is calling to each of us, in the same way. And I like to say it is God calling, "Come on, I'm here, explore me, learn what I am all about. Over here, beloved. Be this. Do this."

I have been called in the past by the gods of writing, movies, drawing, singing, reading, speaking, psychology, traveling, spiritual discipline, and sex. I've learned lessons I didn't expect from each of them, chief among which is that they are all one God. And that each passion carries forward and prepares the place for the next.

Right now, I am dancing, I am tango. It is, and I am wonderful. However, I am not, as yet, a great dancer; I am not even that good, though I will be. I get frustrated, crazy, and discouraged. Nonetheless, I am on this fully engaging, steep learning curve where I get to know nothing — in Zen it's called beginner's mind — and I give myself permission to look stupid and be wrong. But every so often, I have bits of communion with the Divine, stumbling into delight when I stop thinking about doing it right, stop trying to control the dance, and just let go and follow.

The other day, when I was trying to get a certain step I was having so much difficulty with, my dance teacher said to me, "I can lead you through this, but I want you to know what you're doing." How like God, I thought. He doesn't want me to be the mere recipient of his beneficence (wisdom, knowledge, ability, and so on). He wants me to be a fully conscious cocreator in the process. Still, I was tentative. "No," he said, "Not wimpy like that. Be strong." And I said, "Okay, go ahead and be tough on me, I don't mind. I want to learn," and meant it, even through all my whining, sore feet, tiredness, feeling like I was never going to get this. He said, "You haven't seen close to tough yet." And looked amused. So I just said, "Okay," let go, and lo and behold, I could do it. We started to dance the routine we have been working on and I knew what I was doing! I followed him, stayed balanced, strong, loose — perversely in control, and yet perfectly following, and that's when I slipped into the God thing, that ecstasy and bliss we spend so much of our lives avoiding.

You may be in the throes of this madness yourself, or you have been. You may be wondering if it will ever come again or for the first time. It will. You cannot stop it, but you can wait for it to catch up with you. Then all you have to do is make room for the Divine to enter in, by any means possible. It will enter through your enthusiasm, your surrender to, and your obsessive love affair with the ever-expanding heart and mind of God expressing through you, as you.

You have to be willing to give yourself entirely over to the process of learning —something, anything, and it doesn't matter *what, except that you must connect with it on some deep, even inexplicable, level. It must be something challenging and it must be something that takes you out of time and makes you crazy, if only temporarily. You must, in short, fall hopelessly, helplessly, in love with something, anything, and let it reveal your entire life to you. You must let it show you your frailties and your fears. It must cause you pure discomfort and unimagined joy, both the one following on the other rapidly, like tumblers in a circus act. You must know that the impossible thing you are taking on is doable even if you do not as yet know how to do it or even if you don't know why you must.*

The practicalities of life may go unattended from time to time, but your dreams will never go unfulfilled, you will never stop learning, as long as you do this: yearn, reach, stretch out your arms, get yourself up on tippy-toe, don't wimp out, and let God lead you in the dance.

V. YOUNG
SARASOTA, FLORIDA

On Lessons Learned or Not Learned

EILEEN, MY QUICK-WITTED friend with the near incomprehensible, yet lyrical southern Irish Cork accent, writes about what she learned about herself from her dog. Eileen didn't spend years rehabilitating her dog or transforming the way she was. Eileen just accepted herself and her dog, Sasha, the way they were. It was an uneasy sharing of her home that led Eileen to her self-discovery and her ultimate acceptance that she did not have the respect of her dog. You may recognize Eileen and her dog from the first chapter, where she remained anonymous, but her dog, Sasha, and her evil ways were described. Following is Eileen's story in her own words.

I am Eileen, the failed disciplinarian Cindy mentioned in the first chapter. When she showed me what she had written, I was horrified. She had taken all the fun right out of the story! Well, it was funny in spite of the fact that I was terrified that the flyer man would sue me. There was Sasha, sailing four feet into the air to grab the flyers right out of the poor man's hands and then tearing them to shreds. She growled as she went about the serious business of ridding us of the nuisance of flyers, her hackles raised. I'm sure the man was only marginally reassured when I came racing out of the house, my dressing gown flailing behind me, screaming like a mad person.

Sasha has since gone to doggy heaven. My fondest memories of her are not of the times when she behaved perfectly — rare though they were. I loved her outrageousness. She outsmarted me and bullied me at every turn. She bodychecked me into the wall to get to the front door before me. She lounged on the love seat, I sat on the floor. She kept me in shape by eating half my meals. No midnight snack was worth the effort! Oh, there were millions of times that I wished that I could draw cartoons. One night, my hot water bottle leaked and flooded "my" side of the bed. Sasha was in her usual spot — right across the middle of the bed — and she had no intention of moving to accommodate the new reality. I squeezed myself into a dry spot near the wall, straight as a rod. It was so uncomfortable that I seriously debated transferring myself, bag and baggage, into Sasha's large (never used) basket!

By any "normal" person's standards, Sasha's behavior was completely unacceptable. I suppose the truth was that I had long since given up on any hope of changing that behavior, that I was prepared to live my life around her ninety exuberant pounds, and that humor was my only remaining tool.

Life prepared me to be flexible. I was the youngest in a family of four, living in Cork, Ireland. Trying to stay on-side (on any side!) of the ever-shifting alliances of my older siblings required a lot of flexibility and diplomacy. Later, raising two children in a country that was new to me, where my own life experiences were wildly irrelevant, pushed me to become even more flexible. By the time Sasha arrived, I was ripe for exploitation. I might as well have had "pushover" emblazoned across my shirt!

I'm not sure if I have learnt anything new about myself through owning pets, but it has reinforced what I already knew about myself. I am a hopeless disciplinarian; I cannot even discipline myself. "If I treat them well, they will return the favor" does not necessarily work with kids or dogs, though I keep forgetting that. Perhaps most importantly, I have accepted that I am a sucker and that I will never change. After all, is it really that important that I should have a perfectly behaved dog?

My attention is now focused on cats. Yeah, I got suckered into taking in a cat and the three-week-old, sole-surviving kitten she had stopped caring for. But it was supposed to be for three weeks — though I admit that that was over a year ago. Of course, I didn't know that the mother cat was pregnant again and that soon I would have seven cats, all crawling with fleas. By the way, don't you just hate it when the vet's assistant cheerfully talks about your "infestation," advising you to "vacuum every day and throw away the bag"? It all worked out in the end, with Toronto Cat Rescue finding new owners for the kittens once they were old enough to be adopted. And my legs finally did heal from all the scratches of the five newest kittens simultaneously scaling my jeans!

I now have three cats — the mother cat (Her Majesty), that first kitten (Chopper), and my pride and joy from the second litter, Beautiful Belle with the Magnificent Tail. Together, the three of them are hilarious and fascinating. Nobody should have just one cat. Best of all, nobody can blame me for their behavior because the whole world knows that cats are undisciplinable. Of course my cats are spoilt rotten, but it's so much easier to hide!

E. WATSON
TORONTO, ONTARIO

Sometimes Are and Sometimes Not

When Cheryl and her younger sister, Lara, felt increasingly abandoned by their stepfather after the death of their mother, Cheryl came to see me to talk about what she had been learning in her life. Cheryl's stepfather, Peter, had been a wonderful father figure to Cheryl and Lara while they were growing up. He played with them, tickled them, laughed with them, and when their mother was diagnosed with terminal cancer, cried with them and cared for them. Three years after their mother died, Peter met a woman and moved on. He still kept in contact with "his girls," as he called them, but the contact was less and less. Lara had called Peter repeatedly, with no response.

Cheryl had stood back for a few months and realized that her own father had stepped up to the plate recently and had really been there for her. Cheryl had also made several strong friendships with women she met at work. She had recently purchased a house with her boyfriend and was becoming closer with his family. She thought about how people come and go in one's life, and about how Peter had been such a strong presence in her life when she really needed him, but now he had moved on and other people were entering and filling up her life. She acknowledged that she felt deeply sad that Peter was now so distant from her but that she also felt it was right for him. His new wife didn't support him staying in contact with his dead wife's daughters, nor did his new wife understand their need for him.

Cheryl said she wanted to talk to Peter and tell him just how much she loved him for whom he was and for how he was there for her and Lara during their growing-up years. Cheryl wanted to release him from what she believed he felt was his obligation to them as stepdaughters to allow him to move on with his life with his new wife. She also wanted to put an end to her own pain that was caused by her wishing and expecting that Peter still be in their lives. She said quite simply, "I see now that there are times when some people are in your life and times when they are not. This is a time when Peter isn't here, but my father is. It is sad but it is just the way it is, and I have to let go of my expectations of Peter because it hurts me. Peter will always be special in my heart because of what we all went through when my mother was dying. But now he is moving away and I have to let that happen."

Cheryl then told me that she was going to allow her sister Lara to negotiate her own terms with Peter. She said that Lara still needed Peter in her life, and though Cheryl was distressed at the pain it caused Lara when Peter did not respond to her requests for contact, she knew that she had to allow Lara and Peter to work it out in their own way.

I was impressed with Cheryl's clarity about the problem. Cheryl faced the pain of losing her stepfather courageously. She respected and trusted that her stepfather was going through something and was accepting that she had no control over what he was doing and that it had nothing to do with her worth as a stepdaughter. When Cheryl summoned the courage to tell her stepfather what he truly meant to her, she discovered that Peter had been busy with medical tests. He had been diagnosed with cancer.

Lessons in Subtle Courage

THIS IS A STORY FROM one of my friends who had the courage to begin a relationship with a man after she had felt hurt by the end of her marriage and untrusting of men. Though my friend was pushing forward with a man who had shown her he was loving and trustworthy, my friend was full of fear to make the final move. This is her story about how that fear impeded her and affected the innocents in her life.

Ours was a Brady Bunch story of the modern kind. For weeks we postponed the decision to merge the pets in a new blended family. It was like one of those classic statistics problems: two people, two apartments, and three pets with different care requirements.

Jon had Moki, a fifteen-year-old orange tabby recently diagnosed with a pervasive form of cancer (the poor, frail thing). I have Sydney, a six-year-old yellow lab, and Tyson, an eight-year-old Manx. When we were commuting between his and my place, the question was always, which pet should we neglect today? Sadly for the cats, because of the demands of dog walking, we had to alternate ignoring them. The guilt of neglecting one versus another was the worst choice of the Sophie kind (remember the movie Sophie's Choice?). I felt guilty whenever we left one but thought I was doing them a favor by sparing them the trauma of moving in together. Sometimes to be fair to Moki, I left Sydney and Tyson alone overnight and returned in the morning. Leaving the cats was heartbreaking, but leaving the dog was even worse.

For six months I procrastinated with the move, but in the end, exhausted from the commute between his place and my place, Jon and I took the plunge and brought everyone together. Of course we took measures, like easing the dog in by spending short bursts of time at the condo before the move. We also practiced that pet-merge-relationship-management-thing using doors to separate potentially feuding pets.

There were a few tense moments. Sydney versus Moki, Tyson versus Moki, but there were no major incidents. In the end, they all found their place in the pecking order. I even suspect to this day that Sydney and Tyson extended Moki's life by weeks. Moki, ever getting weaker because of cancer, perked right up when the others moved in.

A month after we moved in, Moki died, and Tyson and Sydney provided comfort to both Jon and me. For weeks after, whenever we mentioned Moki's name, Sydney would walk around the place looking for him — in the closet, behind the mirror, behind the chair. I'm glad they had a chance to meet.

The lesson I learnt from this? I should have spared the pets hours of neglect and loneliness. My reluctance to bring them together was more a reflection of my lack of readiness to make a commitment. Should I move in with Jon? Should we combine the pets? I really thought I was doing the cats a favor by leaving them alone for days on end.

All my fears were for naught. They sorted each other out in a hurry. As soon as I made the decision, the pets adapted. Moki was also more resilient than I thought he would be. I gave him too little credit, and I will feel badly about that for a while yet.

Mostly the pet merge taught me the difference between my insecurities and my concern for the pets. I also learnt the price of that indecision. Now that I think about it, if it were me in Tyson, Sydney, or Moki's shoes, and someone gave me a choice between being alone or being with my owner but with other creatures I might not love, I would gladly put up with the others. I wish I had learnt this lesson sooner. Moki would have had a less lonely last few months.

— G. SANCHEZ
VANCOUVER, BRITISH COLUMBIA

Scratch a Dog

SHELLY LOWENKOPF, a great writing mentor and friend, wrote to me about what he learned when asked to write a eulogy for his mother. Though the story seems to be about the desire for immortality, it is a lesson about love, for how else could one create such a magnificent epitaph?

A MOTHER'S LESSON

Scratch a dog and you'll have a satisfied, grateful friend. Scratch a writer and you'll uncover a hidden longing that afflicts us all, regardless of age, gender, place of origin, or even the era in which we were born. I call it the Flaubert Syndrome, but it is something even more insidious than a preoccupation with le mot juste; it involves nothing less than a desire for immortality. This is one reason why having a writer for a friend is risky. We don't merely strive for immortality once or twice; the affliction is with us every time we pick up our pen.

I knew this about myself and comported myself with what I considered proper writerly modesty until the message was borne home to me in the warm, unusual, typically loving way I had come to expect from my mother. To show you what kind of woman she was — I visited her on her ninety-second birthday, concerned for her need to be sedentary thanks to a recently broken hip, concerned even more that her awareness of her increasing loss of short-term memory was costing her, impinging on that great source of dignity she managed so well. "I probably told you this five minutes ago," she began, "but if there is such a thing as an afterlife, your father is going to have a lot to answer for when I track him down." She had, indeed, expressed this sentiment a few minutes earlier, but, as well, she expressed similar sentiments for as long as I can remember. There was little doubt in my mind that she and my father were an item through their entire lifetime together.

The next day, the day after her ninety-second birthday, she took matters into her own hands — she died. In keeping with the traditions of our faith, she was interred within twenty-fours, next to the remains, appropriately enough, of this droll, devoted man who had so much to answer for. In time, it fell to me to provide the epitaph for her marker, and when I thought about this, the words being engraved on a chunk of polished marble, I realized I would deliberately be writing far beyond my own life span for such ages as there are to come in this giddy, glorious sphere we call earth. The usual tributes: "Loving wife, daughter, mother," or another I actually saw somewhere, "Now cavorting with the angels," or even the strikingly saccharine, "At rest at last," were not only abhorrent, they were singularly inappropriate.

Assignment: You have five or six words to commemorate a beloved parent, imparting a sense of her for the ages, sticking to facts, keeping yourself out of the picture.

You write: "All were welcomed at her table."

You can live with that.

S. LOWENKOPF

SANTA BARBARA, CALIFORNIA

The Doors of Perception

WE EXPERIENCE OUR lives through our senses and we understand our lives through our perceptions. The way we relate to our outer reality is dependent on how we perceive things, since we each interpret our experiences differently; the understanding of events in our lives often differ between one another. There is an old Indian story of the four blind men who happened on an elephant which illustrates the limitations of perceptions when you rely exclusively on your own experience to deliver reality. One man experienced the elephant as a snake; he held the elephant's trunk. Another man experienced the elephant as a tree; he held the elephant's leg. Another man experienced the elephant as sharp, like a spear; he held the elephant's tusk. And yet another man experienced the elephant like the rough and withered skin of old worn leather; he touched the elephant's body. All four men were correct within the limitations of their perceptions.

This is how we all go through life, but we think we are seeing the whole and the real picture. Don't be so sure. We may be limited by our blind spots and not realize it. I think it is so important to keep this in mind when dealing with difficulties. The limits of our perceptions influence our inner states, which consequently affect how we behave in our relationships.

Deceptively Simple

THE CONCEPTS IN this book seem to be common sense, simple ideas, but their simplicity is deceptive. For example, it may sound simple that truth is relative according to whose perspective you are looking from, but just try to put that into practice. Simple? Hardly! I have been forever wedded to being right and often righteous about my positions. It takes a lot of work to begin to see things from other viewpoints. People often become polarized over important issues, like a married couple who will argue straight into divorce court as to who loves the other the most.

The concept is simple. Create a great relationship with a dog, horse, mate, child, or friend; do it with courage, trust, respect, and love. But the lessons are deep, unending, and not necessarily easy to put into practice. The lessons can be mapped onto a variety of contexts. What I've learned is that you can find your guru anywhere. Mine happened to be in Harry. The question is, What can we learn from whatever circumstances confront us? Can we look at our own role, not necessarily in what befalls us but in how we react to what befalls us? How we handle our circumstances? Harry is a wonderful teacher to have in this regard. He has helped me to see how power struggles can completely paralyze relationships; how pack-mentality dominates many structures (for example, governments, corporations, and families), even though we pay lip-service to a different type of structure. He helped me to look at circumstances and see what can be learned from them and then have the persistence to see the learning through to the end.

The lessons for teaching Harry, the guru, were also deceptively simple. Teach him to mind his manners, mind his own business, and think. I have been asked, How do you teach a dog to think? Are you ascribing volitional thinking skills to a dog? I have been accused of anthropomorphizing dogs, and of making claims of magic. On the contrary, there was no magic involved. Just hard work. You teach a dog to think by not doing his thinking for him. Charles Eisenmann was one of the first role models for teaching a dog to think. Treat your dog with the utmost of respect. I speak to Harry as though he understands my complex sentences. I am not sure that he does, but he totally understands my intent.

Once on the boardwalk during a very busy afternoon, Harry decided he didn't want to walk on the leash. He grabbed his leash between his teeth and headed towards the beach and the water. I stopped and said to Harry, "If you are going to be silly, I am not going to walk with you." He stopped, his leash still hanging from his mouth, and looked at me quizzically. People began to form around us as they watched me talk to my dog as though he could understand. I was worried because, at this point, Harry was not far in his training and he was given to tearing around the beach with his leash like a mad dog. I reiterated, "Harry, I am not going to walk with a silly dog." He stood transfixed, trying to figure out what I wanted. He knew he wanted to kick his heels up in the sand, but he also wanted to figure out what I wanted. Suddenly, I had affected him enough that it became important what I wanted. He cocked his head. "This is the leash-only area, Harry. You must walk with me here."

Harry walked back to the boardwalk and practically handed me the leash. The people who had stopped laughed and shook their heads with delight at our budding argument and my ultimate victory. Someone said, "Wow, that dog seemed to understand." My heart was beating, as I knew what kind of mad dog Harry could become. I was worried we hadn't come far enough for him to trust my wishes over his own desires. That moment marked another turning point in our relationship.

Harry will always be filled with his Harry-ness. He is a character, with a strong will, a fun-loving spirit, and a mischievousness that can be quite comical. Now, I am confident that I have gained his trust, respect, and love. The fear that characterized so much of our early life together is released, and I can use my courage to do daily battle with my shyness, my insecurities, and maybe even attempt to write that next book that deals with more of the learning that Harry, the incidental guru, continues to teach me. Awareness is my guiding light. I have learned to look for the subtle signs in dog behavior and my own that govern our interactions. Clarity of intent is paramount. The deeper my awareness, the better I am able to understand myself, my dog, and others. The learning never ends, and when it does, so will life.

Process Versus Content

WHEN WE GET caught up in the content of our life lessons, the crisis becomes all-consuming and our emotions rule our minds. We risk missing the opportunity to gain awareness and understanding of our all too familiar patterns in life. We end up paying too much attention to the content and not enough attention to the process. That is why the four elements can become so powerful in learning how to stay out of the content, helping us gain emotional distance from the crisis and giving us a process of how to proceed in the learning.

Do the four-elements checklist: What do I fear? Have courage. What am I avoiding? Find trust. Am I being true? Be respectful. What is my motivation? Be loving.

1. Courage: Have the courage to become self-aware, to be honest, to communicate.
2. Trust: Discover your inner voice and trust it. Trust that you have the capacity to deal with your own lessons and to learn from your lessons. Learn to trust yourself so that you can learn to trust others.
3. Respect: Respect yourself and others.
4. Love: Act in accordance with loving intention. In everything you do, do it with love.

Dark Moments of Crises

THINKING ABOUT THE dark moments of our crises and what we can learn from those crises puts the power into our hands to choose to grow. The more we develop our ability to become aware of ourselves and others, to listen to our own lives, to develop our ability to communicate directly, and to become responsible and accountable, the more likely we are to know fulfillment. During a conversation with a few close friends, we talked about what drives us in our lives. For one, it is happiness; for another, serenity; and for another, security. For me, it is fulfillment. When fulfilled, I feel happy and serene. I am energized to keep moving forward and learn what I need to learn.

On this journey, my understanding continues to grow and to be refined. What seemed absolutely true one day will shift into a deeper understanding and sometimes even a new understanding the next day.

Go with courage headlong into the wind, have trust it will all work out if you heed your lessons, respect the universe, and love as though you've never been hurt.

Suggested Reading

Barks, Coleman, and John Moyne, trans. *The Essential Rumi*. New York: HarperCollins Publishers, 1995.

Bekoff, Marc. "Dog Trust: Deep Lessons in Compassion, Devotion, Respect, Spirituality and Love from Our Loving Companions." www.animalliberty.com.

Bennett-Goleman, Tara. *Emotional Alchemy: How the Mind Can Heal the Heart*. New York: Random House, 2001.

Borovoy, Alan A. *When Freedoms Collide: The Case for Our Civil Liberties*. Toronto: Lester and Orpen Dennys, 1988.

Buber, Martin. *Two Types of Faith*. Translated by Norman P. Goldhawk. New York: Harper and Row, 1961.

Caras, Roger A. *A Dog Is Listening: The Way Some of Our Closest Friends View Us*. New York: Summit Books, 1992.

Carter-Scott, Cherie. *If Life is a Game, These Are the Rules*. New York: Bantam Doubleday Dell Publishing Group, 1998.

Ciaramicoli, Arthur P., and Katherine Ketcham. *The Power of Empathy*. New York: Penguin Books, 2000.

Cleary, Thomas, trans. *I Ching: The Book of Changes*. Boston and London: Shambala Publications, 1992.

Dalai Lama. *Ancient Wisdom, Modern World: Ethics for the New Millennium*. London: Little, Brown and Company, 1999.

Dalai Lama. *The Book of Transformation*. London: Thorsons, 2000.

Dalai Lama. *The Book of Wisdom*. London: Thorsons, 1999.

Davis, Madelaine, and David Wallbridge. *Boundary and Space: An Introduction to the Work of D.W. Winnicott*. New York: Bunner/Mazel, 1981.

Edelman, Hope. *Motherless Daughters*. New York: Dell Publishing, 1995.

Eisenmann, Charles. *Stop! Sit! and Think! The Intellectual Method of Dog Training*. New York: MacDonald-Redmore, n.d.

Epstein, Mark, M.D. *Going to Pieces Without Falling Apart: A Buddhist Perspective on Wholeness, Lessons from Meditation and Psychotherapy*. New York: Random House, 1998.

Fadiman, James, and Robert Frager. *Essential Sufism*. New York: HarperCollins Publishers, 1997.

Ferrini, Paul. *Silence of the Heart: Reflections of the Christ Mind — Part II*. USA: Heartways Press, 1996.

Goodall, Jane, and Phillip Berman (contributor). *A Reason for Hope: A Spiritual Journey*. New York: Warner Books, 1999.

Knapp, Caroline. *Pack of Two: The Intricate Bond Between People and Dogs*. New York: Random House, 1998.

Kohut, Heinz. *The Restoration of the Self*. New York: International Universities Press, 1977.

Kozma, Alex. *Esoteric Warriors*. London and New York: Paul H. Crompton Ltd., 1998.

Marshall Thomas, Elizabeth. *The Social Lives of Dogs: The Grace of Canine Company*. New York: Simon and Schuster, 2000.

McElroy, Susan Chernak. *Animals as Guides for the Soul*. New York: Random House, 1998.

McGraw, Phillip C. *Life Strategies: Doing What Works, Doing What Matters.* New York: Hyperion, 1999.

Miller, Alice. *The Drama of the Gifted Child: The Search for the True Self.* New York: Basic Books, 1994.

Moore, David B., and John M. McDonald. *Transforming Conflict.* Australia: Transformative Justice Australia Pty, 2000.

Moussaieff Masson, Jeffrey. *Dogs Never Lie About Love: Reflections on the Emotional World of Dogs.* New York: Three Rivers Press, Crown Publishers, 1997.

Moussaieff Masson, Jeffrey. *The Emperor's Embrace: The Evolution of Fatherhood.* New York: Simon and Schuster, 1999.

New Skete Monks. *How to Be Your Dog's Best Friend: A Training Manual for Dog Owners.* Boston: Little, Brown and Company, 1978.

Peck, Scott M., M.D. *People of the Lie: The Hope for Healing Human Evil.* New York: Simon and Schuster, 1983.

Perls, Frederick, M.D., Ralph F. Hefferline, and Paul Goodman. *Gestalt Therapy: Excitement and Growth in the Human Personality.* New York: Dell Publishing, 1951.

Reanney, Darryl. *Music of the Mind, An Adventure into Consciousness.* London: Souvenir Press, 1994.

Sapolsky, Robert M. *A Primate's Memoir: A Neuroscientist's Unconventional Life Among the Baboons.* New York: Scribner, Simon and Schuster, 2001.

Stone, Adam C. *Dog Owners Anonymous.* Toronto: Bark Publications, 1997.

Wilhelm, Richard, and Cary F. Baynes, trans. *The I Ching: or Book of Changes.* Princeton, New Jersey: Princeton University Press, 1950.

Zukav, Gary. *The Seat of the Soul.* New York: Simon and Schuster, 1990.